FURNITURE FOR THE 21st CENTURY

FURNITURE
FOR THE
21st CENTURY

Edited by
Betty Norbury

STOBART DAVIES
HERTFORD

DEDICATION

For Ian

"In misery's darkest caverns known,
His ready help was ever nigh."
Samuel Johnson

ACKNOWLEDGEMENTS

I would like to thank all of the designer-makers who have accepted my constant barrage of requests for information and photographs to meet deadlines with good humour; my local postman, Matthew, who has delivered the photographs with care and patience. A special thank you to my publisher, Brian Davies, who has painstakingly brought order to the diverse selection of images and text. I also acknowledge the help of Andrew Varah, Rupert Senior, Simon Channing-Williams, Andrew Mawson, Arthur Andersen and the Worshipful Company of Furniture Makers. A special mention for my husband Ian, who keeps me objective and encourages me constantly.

British Library Cataloguing in Publication Data

A catalogue record for this book is available from the British Library

ISBN 0 85442 077 0

Published 1999 by
Stobart Davies Ltd., Priory House, Priory Street, Hertford SG14 1RN.
Printed in Singapore

Preface

As we enter the new millennium there is a sense of regeneration and a new entrepreneurial spirit emerging in the business, public and voluntary sectors which is changing the face of the country. Society is re-evaluating itself, taking a long hard look at some of its most intractable social problems and exploring the new relationships which are growing out of the partnership culture of the last decade.

Human life and the relationships that we build between each other are profoundly affected by the environment in which we live and work. Build tenement housing blocks with poor quality materials and a squalid environment and do not be surprised when human life does not flourish there. The Bromley by Bow Centre in the heart of the East End of London built a health centre in the form of a cloister with handmade bricks, surrounded by a three acre park and gardens, art and sculpture and few were surprised that human relationships improved at the same time. Clearly, we are a reflection of the environments in which we live. The offices and factories in which we work and the hospitals and schools from which we receive our health care and education profoundly affect us. Design therefore, impacts directly on people's identity, both individually and corporately.

The furniture in this book, custom made by highly skilled individuals, sets the standard against which more mass-produced products will be judged. In real terms this amounts to a counter revolution against the cheap, mass-produced, throw-away values of the post-war period and a return to traditional ideals of craftsman-made, well designed objects, built to last, which provide opportunities to small business, give meaning and identity to the environment for those who live within it, use natural resources prudently and are cost effective in the long run. Major corporations and businesses, public institutions and the more affluent members of society have already seen this truth and are investing in furniture and decoration made by the finest craftsmen. Arthur Andersen understands the importance of quality and design and this company will host a major exhibition featuring the artists in this book on its launch at the Banqueting House on Whitehall, London. The GuildHouse in Stanton, Gloucestershire, now being developed as a centre for social entrepreneurs, is destined to become a show-house for the country's finest craftsmen. The new millennium spirit, focused on high quality outcomes for all, will be instilled throughout society, enriching the lives of every one of us.

Andrew Mawson
Chairman of the Bromley by Bow Centre, Executive Director of the Community Action Network (CAN) and Chairman of the Trustees of the Stanton GuildHouse Trust

Introduction

I can claim no driving force for becoming interested in furniture designer-makers; it has been a happy accident. Twenty years ago when I opened my gallery, tucked away as it is in Cheltenham, it seemed only natural to hold an exhibition in the middle of the town to publicise its location. This was the very first contemporary furniture exhibition I organised; following that, I organised occasional exhibitions, until, encouraged by my husband and the makers in the early '90s, the exhibition 'A Celebration of Craftsmanship' came to be held annually in August in Cheltenham. Over the years I have studied the work and the makers and now I feel I know them. But for me the thrill never goes away; every year as we set up the exhibition I marvel at the perfection of construction, the imaginative way with which they tackle design problems for their clients, the minute attention to details that will never be seen by the casual observer, the tactile quality they achieve with the materials used. There cannot be another body of diverse and disparate people with such a passion for uncompromising dedication to perfection.

With this book I would like to take you, the casual observer, the private or corporate client, the would-be furniture designer-maker, the historian, the student and introduce you to these people and their work so that never again can a furniture historian say 'they don't make furniture like that any more' and remain unchallenged.

To compile this book choices had to be made and opinions other than my own sought. I drew up a core list of furniture designer-makers working in the contemporary scene, whose craftsmanship is without question, and circulated it to everyone on the list, asking them to support it, add to it or subtract from it and make suggestions for those makers who would become a force to be reckoned with in the 21st century. Then, over a three week period, I travelled 2,000 miles visiting workshops and interviewing all the makers suggested. I cut and trimmed, expanded here and there and this is what is now presented to you - in my opinion the best all-round furniture designer-makers in the country. The top makers are each featured on three double page spreads throughout the book. The makers who it is felt will play a major role in the industry's continued growth well into the 21st century are featured on one double page spread each. Their names and addresses are listed in the index.

I have always argued that design is subjective. I have walked around the exhibition in Cheltenham, in which there are over 300 pieces, and listened to visitors tell me how much they dislike a design that I have just sold to someone else. So I make no judgements in this respect and I take delight in pieces that work aesthetically for me, but would never impose my own taste on others. There is a lot of nonsense talked about what is the cutting edge of design. Stephen Bailey put it so well on the radio one Sunday in 1998 when he said that in the '40s and '50s fashion designers were predicting that at the end of the century we would all be wearing tight fitting silver space suits and plastic bootees, and we are not. That is the way I feel about this book. Whilst such attention-seeking, way-out designs may have their place in academic or historic tomes, this publication reflects my belief that the vast proliferation of furniture designers/makers in this country in recent years is indicative of an increasing awareness that it is possible to create a more individual living and working space, and that one is no longer compelled to accept what is on offer in the High Street. Within their own budgets, people are making a stand, whether they buy pots of vibrant, coloured paints to cover their walls, or employ a top architect to design an office. Personalised, quality space for leisure and work is rapidly becoming the mood for the 21st Century. These furniture makers delight in the challenges set by their clients and many refer to themselves as problem solvers; they enjoy working in close harmony with the client. Their aim is to design and make furniture to fulfil their requirements ensuring that the client will return, and will recount the pleasure and satisfaction they have had to friends and colleagues. "We will design and make something for them which is more than they could have imagined before they came to the door." was the way Nicholas Dyson expressed this interaction during our interview.

To satisfy a diverse clientele, widely ranging designs will abound; the solutions will be of today and tomorrow, moving inexorably forward, many to become classics of this period. There are no outlandish pieces to astonish and ridicule the observer into thinking that it is they who are in some way deficient, that it is they who lack the education and understanding to appreciate the abstruse qualities so apparent to the art critic. Of all the pieces illustrated in the book, I cannot guarantee what percentage you will love, like, be indifferent to or hate, but what I can guarantee is that the workmanship of every piece is beyond question, beyond average, beyond sufficient, beyond the imagination of anybody else but another furniture designer-maker. For me, the two disciplines are inextricably linked - that of design and fine craftsmanship. As the late David Pye said so many years ago, a badly made piece of work is like a beautiful piece of music badly played. Why would you do it? What would be the point?

If you are unfamiliar with the world of the furniture designer-maker, and this book whets your appetite for ownership of the real thing, then its objectives have been achieved. Whilst it is always possible to buy speculative pieces, commissioning can be a very exciting and fulfilling experience in which one can work creatively with the designer. Putting forward one's own ideas and requirements and watching as they are shaped and honed by an expert into a superb piece of furniture; bringing to fruition simply a bookcase to fill an awkward niche or a stunning writing desk that contains elements that are significant only to you. A unique heirloom that will be passed down through the family.

At the end of the introduction to my first book 'British Craftsmanship in Wood' I expressed a heartfelt desire that when seeking a new piece of furniture a client should not consider '...antique or mass produced?' but rather 'antique, mass produced or craftsman made?' And imperceptibly the tide is turning. As we move into the 21st century the principles that these highly skilled and dedicated designer-makers have adhered to so uncompromisingly are being recognised as valid, and in tune with the times, the environment and the needs of a population satiated with wasteful consumerism.

*   *   *

Sotheby's auction room: a sale of fine antiques is in progress. Lot 237 - a set of six mahogany ribbon back dining chairs and two carvers - 1742 from the workshops of Thomas Chippendale - master cabinet maker - author of the 'Directory of Furniture' etc. etc. Beautiful furniture, warm glowing wood, fine patina, useful, comfortable, the pinnacle of furniture making some would say, hand made. But whose hand? – Not Thomas Chippendale's - he was principally a designer and a businessman. When his workshop burnt down his insurance claim included the tool chests of up to 35 cabinetmakers. Even allowing for the exaggerations of insurance claims, Thomas

Chippendale was a factory - a sweatshop perhaps. So what did all these tradesmen do? Were they stood at a bench making a chair or table? Probably not. More likely, one was sawing out cabriole legs, while another carved them, another sanded and polished them, another cut the joints, another fitted the rails and so on. An 18th century production line? Not entirely. Somewhere was a master cabinet maker (Thomas Chippendale) who orchestrated the whole thing, knew what was needed, altered this and that, controlled quality etc., could alter a design at a moment's notice.

Time went by - industrialisation came to pass. Where the pit saw had been - two men sweating their guts out with a seven foot saw and a log - the power saw relentlessly sliced up trees - circular saws, bandsaws, fretsaws, automatic lathes, woodcarving machines - most of the woodcarving in the Houses of Parliament was done on machines - tireless engines of industry - planing, sanding, mortising - where before there had been a man with a mallet and a chisel.

This was the Victorian achievement. Cheap, nasty furniture made in back street factories, using cheap labour, child labour, in appalling, dangerous conditions. It became a symbol of everything that was shoddy and suspect. Many criticised the poor quality of British manufactured goods and the architect Pugin related the moral state of the nation to the quality of its products. He advocated a return to a more spiritual society and a medieval concept of craftsmanship, where the artisans had some freedom of expression through their work. This ideal was embraced by William Morris, followed by C. R. Ashby and the craft guilds. The Arts and Crafts Movement reverted to manual skills - 'making honest furniture for ordinary folk' – but which only the bourgeois could afford. But still on a business like scale, Morris and Ashby employed dozens, in fact hundreds, stamping out handmade wallpaper and silver jewellery. And then the high point of the Arts and Crafts epoch - The Barnsleys, Ernest Gimson, Romney Green - the new Thomas Chippendales - designing furniture, houses, the whole works. Designing and making to their own moral and aesthetic agenda, some of them actually getting their hands dirty and acquiring blisters. Sadly, by the First World War the Arts and Crafts Movement had become so amateurish, rural and unrealistic that architects and interior designers were reluctant to use its products and in effect it died out. And so industrialisation gathered pace: plywood and plastic and spray varnish; and lurking about in dusty corners, Peter Waals, Edward Barnsley and Stanley Davies carrying the anachronistic torch of the true artisan. For the craftsmen – Chippendale's craftsmen - had become middlemen, albeit indispensable ones. In the mechanised, gear-wheeled, line-shafted, robotic world of mass production, he made the prototype - the designer designed it, the craftsman made it in 3D, sorted out the problems - and the technician geared up the machines to bang them out by the thousands. Today, even this position has been subverted by electronic simulation. With the Second World War the craftsman had a bit of a heyday making propellers and so on, but after the war the factory reigned supreme. Plywood was furniture and furniture was plywood. even when designed by Gordon Russell. Post-war furniture was and still is appalling, but it was all that was available. But beneath it all, like malaria, waiting for another bout, the craftsman furniture maker, men like Hugh Birkett, Edward Barnsley and Oliver Morel.

After the austerity of post-war Europe and the plethora of plastic and vinyl and chrome came a new age of bourgeois affluence when a small part of the population who had money decided they would like something that was half-way decent in their home. Most of them plumped for the ultimately acceptable antiques - money in the bank - the fashionably cheap, stripped pine or a rag-bag of other pseudo-quality furnishings as specified by popular magazines. But a few, a very few, went to the craftsman furniture maker and bought real furniture, made with real wood by someone who cared. Slowly, starting with men like Alan Peters and John Makepeace the craft began to revive.

The situation as it exists, as we enter the new millennium, looks bright. Training centres for fine cabinet making are abundant - one might say too abundant - quality varies and motivation for embarking on a course is not always of the highest level. However, we now enjoy the benefit of a society in which there are hundreds of well trained, highly skilled and for the main part, ethically right-minded, independent furniture makers. This implies a future where many people will commission custom made furniture as readily as they order a fitted kitchen or a set of curtains. Not many years ago, most men who wanted a good suit had it tailor-made. This was a perfectly ordinary function. This is no longer so. Most men under the age of forty have never had that experience. But by the same token, before the seventies, many ordinary people who had never eaten in restaurants, would now be reluctant to drag themselves away from the T.V. to visit one, so 'everyday' has it become.

Society changes rapidly and huge proportions of the public are carried along by fashion or the passing fad. There is every indication that there is a growing disillusionment with universal industrialisation and the production line goods offered by it. They are no longer seen as acceptable - the individual wants to assert his individuality, hence the plethora of designer labels, special editions, the huge prices paid for 'personalised' car licence plates, and so forth. Many of these fashions - notably those in clothing are created by high profile designers whose ideas change the world practically overnight. This to me is one of the great weaknesses of many furniture designer-makers - they are by nature low profile, self-deprecating, avoiding the limelight. Like their ancestors of the Arts and Crafts Movement they shut themselves away in the countryside amid the trappings of 'tradition'. At the present, this comfortable ambience is not seen as 'Where it's at - Where things happen'. Time, I believe, will reveal to the public that the life style of these makers, their isolated dedication to their work and unremitting commitment to quality and integrity go hand in hand with the financial and environmental incentives of the rural scene. There seems no reason why these makers should not continue in the 21st century and become world leaders in the genre of hand-made furniture.

What then, is the driving force of this dramatic rise of the designer-maker? It would be very convenient to be able to say that industrially made furniture is all chipboard rubbish that falls to bits the day after the guarantee runs out. Unfortunately, modern production techniques are so sophisticated that 'craftsman' quality really can be guaranteed on a mass production scale. And at the top end are probably just as expensive as the hand made product.

So what is the difference? Giuseppe Chigiotti, lecturer on Morphology of Components at the Faculty of Architecture in Florence, points out in 'Il Neoeclettismo 1993-4' that until recently craftsmen-made products were distinguished by the ability to intervene at any time during production and alter any aspect of the product. Thus, the principles of mass production were totally foreign to the principles of the craftsman. However, modern mass production systems are so sophisticated that to a large extent they can intervene in the process and so emulate those of the craftsman. The distinction therefore, between the craftsman and industry, given that industry can produce the same levels of manufacturing perfection, is between the 'one-off custom-made' article and the hand-made article. What they share is the unrepeatable experience of a trial and error process where the object is commissioned without being seen or tested. This is the principle of 'made to measure'. This link between designer, craftsman and user is the traditional relationship, universally understood to produce the very highest quality, unique work. Chigiotti states "This complex of attitudes has led to the idea of the negative nature of the copy as opposed to the exceptional nature of the one-of-a-kind piece, often distinguished by virtuosity of execution." It is the personal touch, the appeal to the individuality of the buyer, the personal statement about 'my home', 'my office', 'my space'.

However, Chigiotti carries on to say although modern production systems have rendered obsolete the concept of being unable to intervene in a pre-set programme, any intervention must still be programmed 'a priori' before it can take place. Even now, only the craftsman can make alterations on a whim. This necessity for 'a priori' programming is still a controlling factor. Chigiotti concludes "Moreover, in such a context there is no osmosis or process of integration between the consumer and the producer, apart from the acceptance or rejection of the final product".

No longer restrained by financial imperatives, the modern homeowner demands more than a furnished space to live in, no matter how fashionable or trendy. He wants a home in which he has decided to live not only by means of the 'virtual nature of image', but which includes the 'material nature of objects'. His dining room may not be essentially a place for eating, but for communicating with friends, his lounge may be a computer centre, his bathroom a gymnasium. His home, and possibly his office, is his personal space and ideally would be tailored to his personal requirements. The production line cannot cater for him, his requirements are not, literally, 'run of the mill'. Nor is this merely a practical consideration. In a home, every object has a memory - an inherited mirror, a junk shop chair, a rug from a holiday in Turkey, etc. etc. But a factory made dining table has the same memory as a fridge or a microwave. A piece of furniture from a designer/maker implies a deep involvement in the commissioning process - a two-way consultation - How long? How high? What wood? Which finish? It carries with it the life and experience of the maker, his design ideas, his environmental considerations, his labour, his love, the nature of the material and his treatment of them and his interaction with the client. At the end of the day, a unique object, a product of maker and client.

This symbiotic relationship is equally apparent in the corporate field, which many of the designer-makers tend to specialise in. There is no shortage of companies keenly aware of their image, both to the public and to other companies. Hand-made furniture can now be seen as museum and atrium seating, boardroom tables and chairs, reception areas, even in the ubiquitous hamburger restaurant. The message going out is that companies who think a little bit further than the profit and loss columns care about how they are perceived - and once again the intrinsic, implied good ethos of the one-off hand-made object is telling, the tacit suggestion that this company is one of quality, and that quality is reflected in all it does - not least the furnishing of the buildings. Those wishing to make a stand on environmental issues can take comfort that most furniture designer-makers share their concerns for wildlife habitats, rain forests, energy conservation and pollution - indeed many of them are experts on the subject and work within a rigorous regime of self-discipline, refusing to use materials they cannot totally approve of.

As we enter the new millennium the world-wide feeling of optimism that is growing seems somehow inextricably linked with technology, and yet, on consideration, one can hardly avoid the conclusion that it is technology that is failing the world, causing destruction and pollution of the planet. Most of that technology is dedicated to supplying the demand of an insatiable consumerism, which is in turn engendered and fostered by the manufacturing industry. Whilst it may be too much to hope that this whirlpool may be halted, there are encouraging signs that the more perceptive among the population are trying to contribute less to the merry-go-round and make at least a token effort towards improving the world by demanding a minimum of moral standards in the manufacturing process of the goods they purchase - that is 170 years after Pugin suggested it.

I believe that in the new millennium, more and more people will want a better environment, a better living space, and perhaps more important, will see that it is not enough just to improve their own ivory tower - the environment of those less financially comfortable than themselves must also be looked to if the spiritual welfare of society is to be bettered. I believe this book is the future of furniture making, and the makers I have chosen are those who have led the crusade - those who are carrying the flag and some of those who will take it up and carry it forward in the 21st century.

Betty Norbury, August 1999

Matthew Burt

"I am endlessly delighted and increasingly fascinated by the joy of selling beautifully made and enduring pieces of furniture to individuals"

Matthew Burt

Matthew Burt's work is rooted in English country furniture, fertilised by the Shaker style and pruned by modernism. His overwhelming enthusiasm and pleasure in using wood appropriately, making fine furniture and creating beautiful objects that will become treasured family heirlooms, is only eclipsed by his determination to perform the daunting task of doing this for ordinary people at affordable prices.

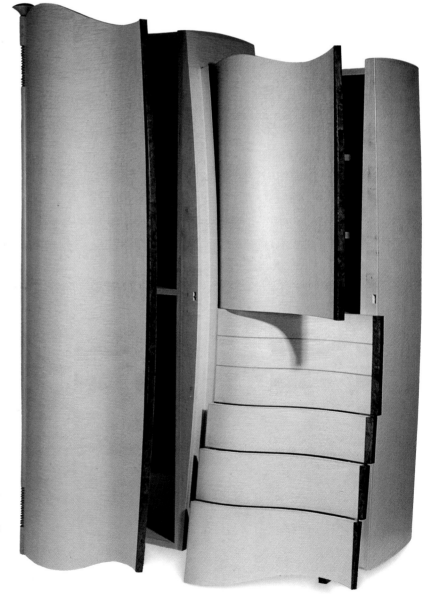

Banner Wardrobe
Ripple sycamore and cedar with burr elm details.
2110 x 1520 x 690mm / 83 x 60 x 27 in.

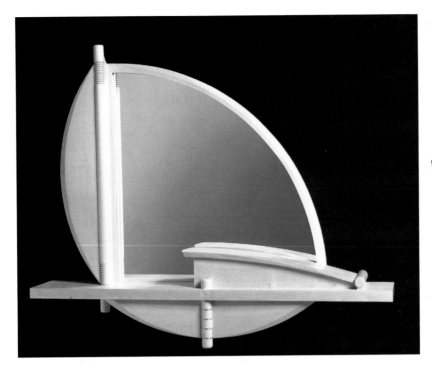

'Before You Go' hallway organiser

Mirror with key cabinet to its side. The horizontal shelf supports on
its upper face a box with a lid that pivots upwards; on its under
surface hang two drawers that swing outward from a central pivot.
980 x 1150 x 150mm / 38 x 45 x 6 in.

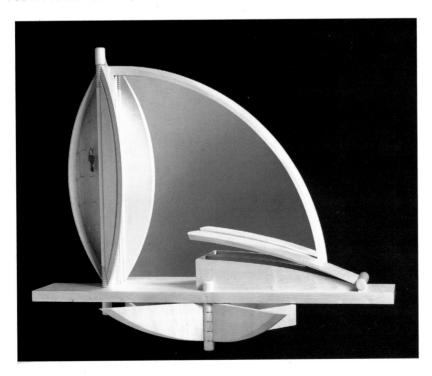

Reading chair with removeable book holder
Sycamore and walnut.

Desk
Two drawers either side of frame; top box with
three drawers. Sycamore, stainless steel and
powder-coated aluminium.
760 x 2000 x 900mm / 30 x 78 x 36 in.

Dining table and 'Tricorn' upholstered chairs
Diamond pattern sycamore with walnut line.

Detail of dining table

'Tricorn' chairs in ash

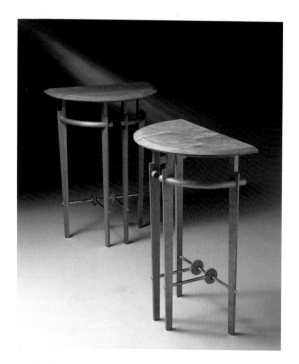

Occasional table
Cherry and brass
820 x 630 x 360mm / 36 x 25 x 14 in.

CD lozenge
Lacewood. Holds 60
compact discs.
800 x 200 x 170mm / 32 x 8 x 7 in.

Low fan table   Walnut and bronze.   410 x 1470 x 1880mm / 16 x 58 x 74 in.

Intimate seat with integral table and sculpted seats
Oak and brass

Partner's table and tambour lockers
The tables can be joined as one unit or broken up into three independent ones. Each has integral cable storage shown at the centre of the table top. Beech.
Each table: 740 x 1660 (longest arc) to 1070 (inner arc) x 1295mm
29 x 65 to 42 x 51 in.

Ashley Cartwright

Bench for two
Chestnut with coloured metal structural elements. The wide arms are for resting drinks.
1650mm / 65 in.

Ashley Cartwright's wide academic training, his international reputation as an advisor and adjudicator in design, and his vast experience at home and abroad in the field of furniture making and environmental design have placed his name at the forefront in publications, exhibitions and commissions for the past thirty years. Despite, or perhaps because of, his exceptional knowledge of his subject, his furniture is simple, based on an analysis of balance and form, virtually undecorated and constructed of plain home grown timbers, mostly made to commission, for clients who are heavily involved in the design and making process.

Seat

One of a series of seats in oak with galvanised metal structure. The detail right, shows the subtle shape of the edging.

Long Bench

With 24 legs of round cut sycamore. 3000mm / 118 in.

Table
Limed oak, with zigzag
decoration.
1500mm / 59 in.

Low table
Ash, with tapering edge.
900 x 900 x 400mm / 35 x 35 x 16 in.

Side table
Limed oak, with chevron cut
edge. Detail shown below.
1500 x 400 x 850mm high
59 x 16 x 33 in.

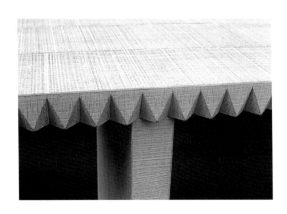

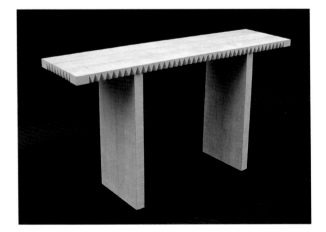

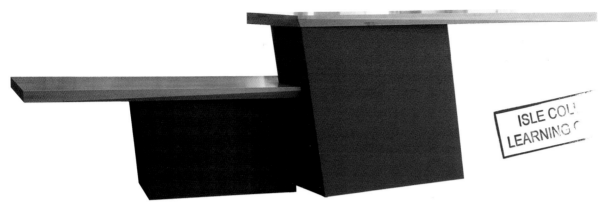

Reception Desk in maple

For the City of Birmingham Symphony Orchestra.
4500mm / 177 in.

Detail

Shows surface edge and juxtaposing planes.

Sideboard

Six curved doors overlap each other when opened. Inside are seven drawers and shelving. Pearwood.
1800 x 900mm / 71 x 35.5 in.

Detail

Shows drawer handles.

Oak dining table
The oak for this table originated from the Royal Botanical Gardens, Kew ,
Surrey. The original tree plaque is set into the table structure. Seats twenty.
5500 x 1000mm / 216 x 39 in.

Detail
Shows underframe
structure.

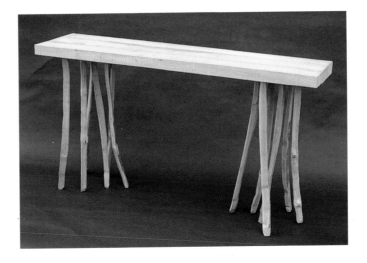

Small side table (left)
Sawn beech with cleft chestnut legs.   500mm / 20 in.
Side table (above)
Sawn elm with cleft chestnut legs.   1500mm / 59 in.
Side table (below)
Sawn elm with cleft ash legs.   2200mm / 86 in.

Cato

"If you walk into a room that has a beautiful piece of furniture - you could say the same of a stunning work of art, even a superb rug, anything - there is definitely something that emanates from that which contributes to the atmosphere in the home."

Tony Portus

Seven years working in management for one of the early life-style retailers convinced Tony Portus that furniture could be better designed and made than that being imported. Thus motivated, he went to Parnham College, later setting up his own workshop in the early eighties. He feels that furniture should be more than an object, it should be a presence in the room. His objective is to instil a sense of peace and calm.

'Elevata'
Shelving in maple and cast aluminium. Elliptical shelves that can be positioned at any height, sliding on a single wall post.
1800 x 750 x 450mm / 71 x 30 x 18 in.

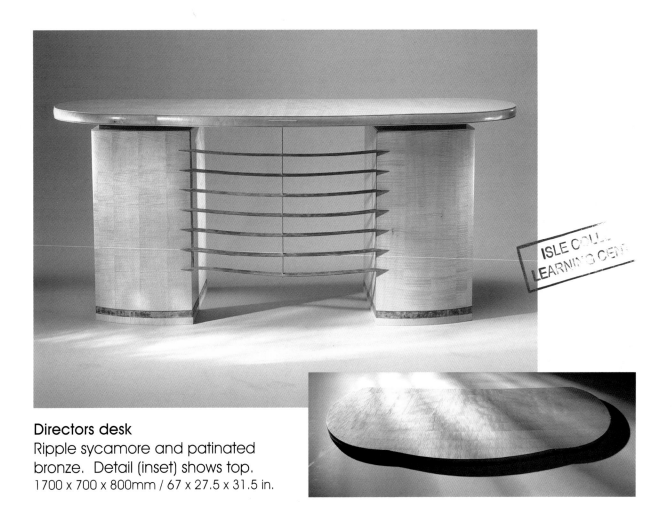

Directors desk
Ripple sycamore and patinated
bronze. Detail (inset) shows top.
1700 x 700 x 800mm / 67 x 27.5 x 31.5 in.

'Plateau'
A low table in
sycamore. Its
concealed metal
bracing allows the
top and legs to
meet at a fine
edge.
1100 x 700 x 360mm
43 x 27.5 x 14 in.

'Towers'
Wall furniture in quilted maple. These cabinets, which are pierced by a single narrow shelf, provide drawers, shelves, cupboards and roll top drinks cabinet.
2100 x 3000 x 700mm
83 x 118 x 28 in.

Fan Screen or room divider
Walnut with removeable silk panels.
1700 x 3000 x 400mm
67 x 118 x 16 in.

'Cato Rocker'
Maple.
950 x 750 x 850mm / 37 x 30 x 33 in.
(Co-designed with Patrick Stronach)

'Beam' cabinet

Five double-fronted drawers,
mitred into the cabinet to give a
seamless 'beam'. English oak.
2500 x 700 x 400mm / 98 x 28 x 16 in.

Console table

The legs, elliptical in section,
scorched and waxed, support a
polished oak top. English oak.
900 x 1100 x 400mm / 35 x 43 x 16 in.

Bedroom cabinet
One of three matching cabinets internally fitted with drawers, shelving and hanging rail. Veneered in yew with a sycamore interior.
2350 x 760 x 440mm
93 x 30 x 17 in.

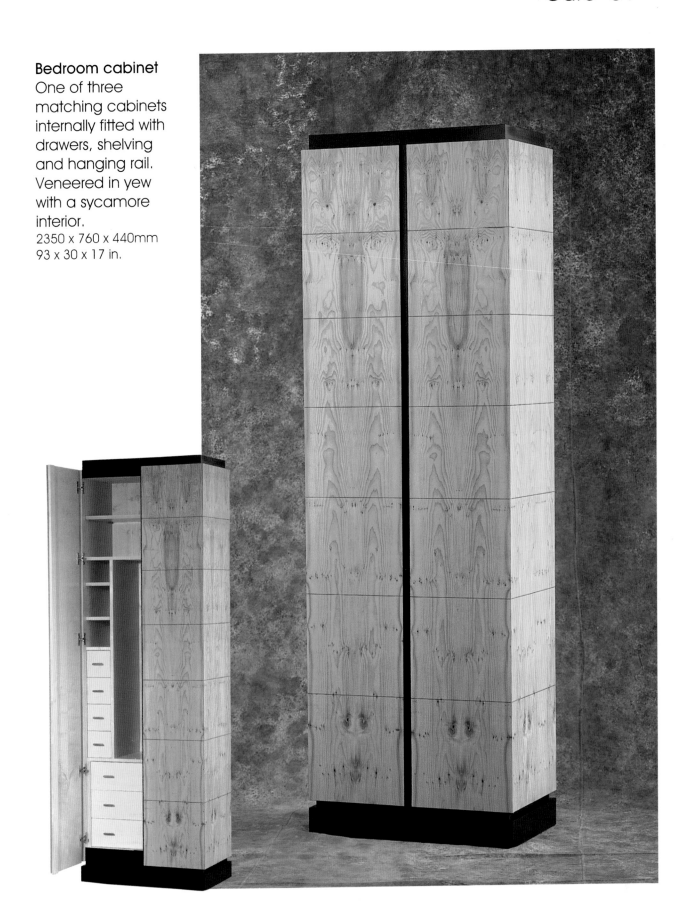

John and Louise Cropper

As a husband and wife team, John and Louise Cropper have been making furniture for many years, but operating mainly as makers for other designers. Their craftsmanship is of the highest standard and highly respected in the trade. However, although still keeping a low profile and seldom exhibiting, they are now beginning to make an impact as designer-makers in their own right.

'Shapes' cabinet in burr veneers
Fourteen shaped units to store the usual requirements for the home office.
2030 x 1070 x 510mm / 80 x 42 x 20 in.

'Jigsaw' bookcase
A variety of interlocking pieces of wood.
1520 x 1000 x 350mm / 60 x 39 x 14 in.

Hall table and mirror

Olive ash burr veneers with masur birch were used to create an 'aged' effect for this piece. The details below show the use of dyed veneers for the marquetry ivy that grows across the table top and face of the frame.

Table: 860 x 910 x 410mm / 34 x 36 x 16 in.
Mirror: 915 x 610mm / 36 x 24 in.

"Constant attention to detail must be applied at every stage of the process, from the very first meeting with the client to the delivery of the piece. There is no opportunity for slackness at any stage."
Gordon Russell

Detail

Although trained as a furniture maker as well as a designer Gordon Russell now spend his time solely designing, drawing his inspiration, he tells me, from the sensuality of the female form. The making facility at Detail was closed in 1996 and it is now done by carefully chosen makers in their own workshops. Gordon's company is aptly named because it is the constantly monitoring of the minutiae to produce the quality he wants that is all-important to him.

'Reflections of a hoarder'
Deep cut solid bird's eye maple. The full length mirror is pivoted and the doors become shelves in the open position.
2000 x 600mm / 79 x 24 in.

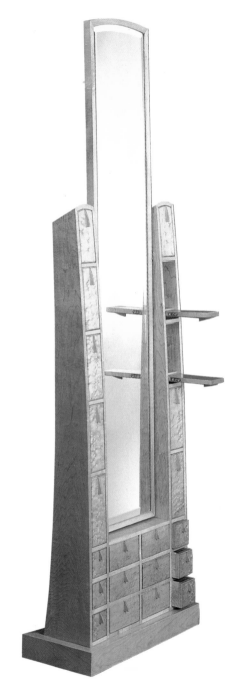

Child's cot

Designed in homage to the Glasgow style. The shaped framework is in American cherry with blue glass.

'Bordello chaise'

Upholstered in cherry cotton velvet. The nozzle has been gold leafed while the studs are in polished brass and the legs in steamed beech.
900 x 2200 x 900mm / 35 x 87 x 35 in.

'Reynolds' dining table and 'Queens' chairs
The table has a drop leaf and swing legs. Solid maple, cast aluminium and blue glass. Chairs with tan leather upholstery.
1800 x 1000mm / 71 x 39 in.

Dining table and chairs
Table in solid English oak with cast iron 'shoes' and bolt heads. Seats eight. Dining chairs are mild steel with a bronzing solution etched on the surface. Horns and feet are in oak to match the table.
2200 x 1000mm / 87 x 39 in.

'Redwing' table
Circular glass top with stained MDF.
Shoes and nipples in aluminium.
1200mm / 47 in. diameter

Crescent dresser
Steamed beech and nickel
plated steel. The mirror is
supported on twin
gooseneck supports allowing
full flexibility of movement.
1800 x 500mm / 71 x 31 in.

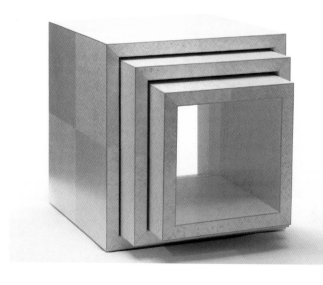

Nest of cubes
Made in alpi-lignum with solid
boxwood edge details. The grain
direction alternated to effect a
harlequin impression around the
faces.
Largest cube: 600mm / 24 in.

Boardroom
The table is finished in a polyester resin and the 'lily' chairs are fully upholstered. Glass panels have been etched to echo the design of the nearby reception area.
The table: 3000 x 1100mm / 118 x 43 in.

Home study with storage cabinet
Interior storage features suspension filing and adjustable shelving. The desk has hollow back legs for cable access to the management disc in the top. American white oak and cast iron.

Detail 39

Hall storage units

Wardrobe storage for a studio flat. All elements work individually as well as grouped together. Vavona, cast aluminium and blue glass.

'Slotted diner'

Tall backed dining chair upholstered in black leather with solid oak frame.

Waddesdon desks

The desks have cable management facilities along the back edge under bronze flaps. Black desk top lino with solid English oak.
6600mm / 21ft 6 in.

Nicholas Dyson

"We will design and make something for our clients which is more than they could have imagined before they came to the door."
Nicholas Dyson

Nicholas Dyson only occasionally works at the bench these days, preferring the rapid pace of designing for his busy workshop where his ideas can advance more quickly. It was several years ago that he made the deliberate decision to build up the corporate side of his business, targeting interior designers and architects who were able to draw on the greater resources of large organisations to furnish their boardrooms and offices. However, he still welcomes private clients and enjoys the particular satisfaction that comes with these commissions.

Tub chair
Walnut and maple.

Bucket seat
Maple frame, upholstered seat and a
moulded ply back faced with wenge.

'Shrimp' low tables
Beech legs with coloured
lacquer tops.
500mm / 20 in. diameter

'Oyster' low table
Beech legs with coloured
lacquer top with glass insert
and under shelf.
1500mm / 59 in. diameter

Desk
A simple construction sets off striking
geometric forms accentuated by
contrasting materials. Pear, walnut,
maple and nickel-plated steel.
2200 x 1100 x 730mm / 87 x 43 x 29 in.

Three-sided conference table and chairs

Table in walnut and grey dyed veneers. The detail right, shows side and armchairs in walnut, ripple ash and horsehair fabric upholstery.

Table: 2400 x 2080mm / 94 x 82 in.

Boardroom table
and **detail** of table support.
To seat twenty. Reconfigures
into two separate tables.
Pear, walnut and burr walnut.
Assembled dimensions:
9000 x 2000mm / 29ft 6 in. x 6ft 6 in.

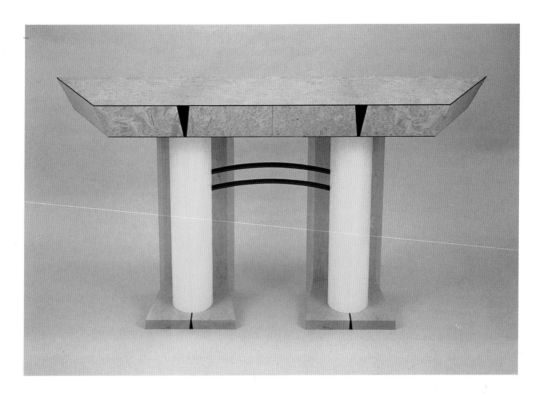

Console table
Maple, burr maple, ripple
sycamore and black steel.
1800 x 600mm / 71 x 24 in.

'Ivory' table and chairs
Ash
1800 x 1200 x 720mm / 71 x 47 x 28 in.

Sean Feeney

Folding screen
Cocobolo, ash and mother of pearl.
2000 x 1800mm / 79 x 41 in.

Whatnot
Ash, cocobolo and glass.
1800 x 1200 x 500mm / 71 x 47 x 20 in.

Sean Feeney pursued woodwork and design skills through school in Sussex and further education at Rycotewood College, followed by three years of further study in a design consultancy and furniture makers in Warwickshire before setting up his own workshop in 1979. Now well established, Sean's output is small, ten to twelve pieces of furniture a year. He exhibits rarely, does not advertise and works with one assistant in an old school house tucked away in the Warwickshire countryside. Relying confidently on word-of-mouth for all of his clients he complains only of there not being enough hours in the day to achieve all his ambitions.

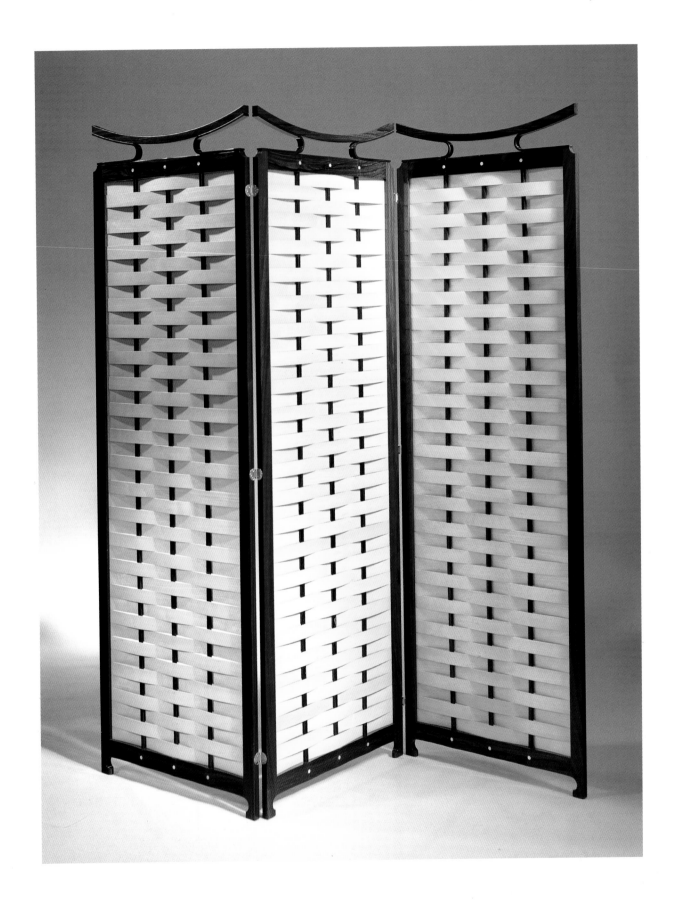

Low table
Burr elm and Cameroon ebony.
460 x 1200 x 600mm / 18 x 47 x 24 in.

Pier table
Burr elm with sycamore and
ebony stringing.
1000 x 800 x 460mm / 39 x 31 x 18 in.

Pair of low tables
Macassar ebony and
sycamore with cherry inlay.
600 x 600 x 460mm / 24 x 24 x 18 in.

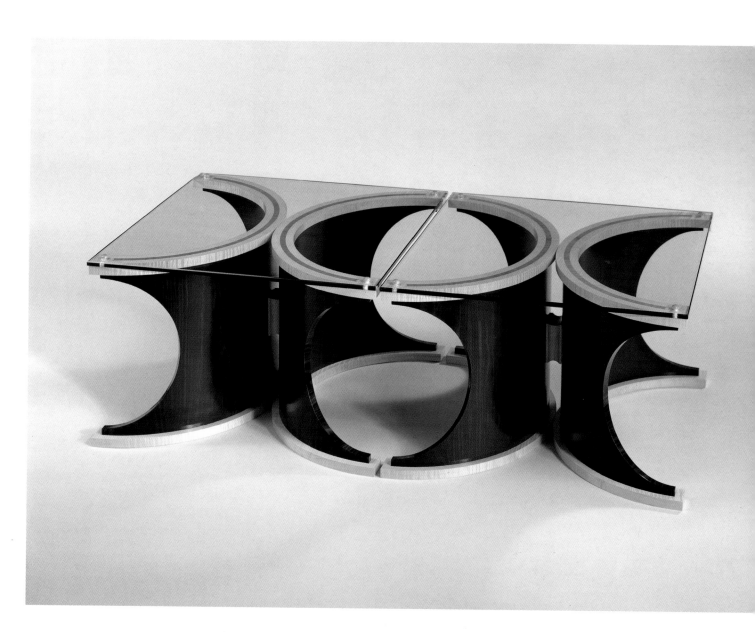

50 Sean Feeney

Dining table
Burr elm and oak with
sycamore and ebony
inlay.
2133 x 915mm / 84 x 36 in.

'Strad' compact disc cabinet
The faux table with hinged
single door encloses a
compartmentalised interior.
Sycamore and rosewood.
800 x 460 x 200mm / 31 x 18 x 8 in.

Breakfront sideboard
Ripple sycamore and burr elm,
with oak lined drawers.
1100 x 460 x 900mm / 43 x 18 x 35 in.

'Delta' desk
Burr elm and wych elm.
2000 x 1000 x 770mm / 79 x 39 x 30 in.

Paul Gower

"I need pieces of wood around. They create the ideas - combinations of forms, shadows and textures - the sources are many. I can walk into an engineering workshop and find inspiration for a little ball handle from a high pressure nozzle, and that to me is exciting - not sitting down with a piece of paper and trying to take a new look at something that has already been done."
Paul Gower

'Skyline' cabinet
Ripple maple and
stainless steel.
1190 x 520 x 600mm
47 x 20 x 24 in.

'Square Peg' table (above)
Bleached English oak.
730 x 1750 x 550mm / 29 x 69 x 22 in.

'Skyline' desk
Ripple maple.
730 x 2000 x 910mm / 29 x 79 x 36 in.

David Gregson

Tower of drawers
Burr elm, ebony and copper.
1220 x 600 x 550mm / 48 x 24 x 22 in.

David Gregson was a portrait painter, and having made a few pieces of furniture for his home, decided this had to be a more satisfying way of making a living. This fanciful idea was fuelled by a visit to an exhibition of contemporary furniture. He had no prior knowledge of furniture, tailor-made for a client to fulfil a particular set of parameters, nor any concept of the very high standard of work on offer. David was hooked and has striven ever since to achieve and ultimately surpass the level of design and craftsmanship that was displayed.

Table (above)
Bleached and limed elm with copper inlay.
1220mm / 48 in. diameter.

Table
Elm.
1530 x 600mm / 60 x 24 in.

Blanket chest with tray
Bleached and limed elm,
cedar of Lebanon, wenge
and copper.
480 x 1070 x 610mm / 19 x 42 x 24 in.

Wardrobe
Bleached and limed elm,
wenge and copper.
1980 x 1140 x 640mm / 78 x 45 x 25 in.

Tower of drawers
Bleached and limed elm,
wenge and copper.
1220 x 600 x 550mm / 48 x 24 x 22 in.

Sideboard and mirror
Maple.
750 x 1350 x 450mm
30 x 53 x 18 in.

Portable lectern
Made for Norwich
Cathedral in cherry.
1365 x 850 x 575mm
54 x 33 x 23 in.

Desk and chair
Maple, brown oak,
apple wood and
ebony.
760 x 1500 x 730mm
30 x 59 x 29 in.

Foyer seating (Left)
Designed and made for the University of East Anglia.
Bleached and limed elm, carved ash and stainless
steel.
460 x 1220mm / 18 x 48 in. diameter, and 460 x 2060 x 400mm / 18 x 81 x 16 in.
Single bench below: 460 x 3960 x 400mm / 18 x 156 x 16 in.

Garden bench in oak (below)
990 x 1850 x 580mm / 39 x 73 x 23 in.

Martin Grierson

Martin Grierson has strong traditional roots: having been good at both art and woodwork since the age of eight, he was encouraged to combine both of these interests in a career. He attended the Central School of Arts and Crafts and spent five years in architectural offices before setting up his own design consultancy. His own workshops came later out of a desire to see his work better made.

"I think the future is very encouraging because the advantage of the designer-maker over manufacturing industry is that every job is different: you have a different person to design for, different building, different interior design - whatever it is - and you can respond to each job. You can do this in a way that no manufacturer could ever do."
Martin Grierson

Collector's cabinet on stand
Macassar ebony.
1400 x 500mm / 55 x 20 in.

Boardroom table and chairs
Made for the St Bride Foundation Institute. The table is modular
and can be folded to stand round the walls as console tables
and assembled in other shapes. English and French walnut.
3000 x 5000mm / 10 x 16 ft.

Gentleman's dressing chest
Weathered sycamore and
pear with rosewood handles.
1100 x 960mm / 43 x 38 in.

Bookcase
Solid American black walnut
with silver inserts in handles.
1560 x 1750mm / 61 x 69 in.

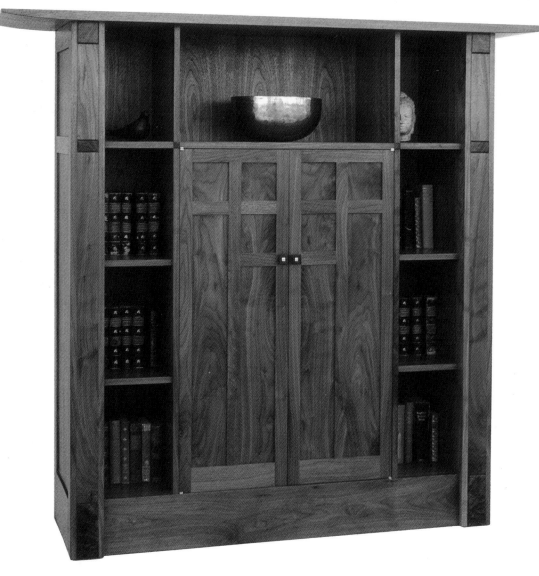

Dining table, chairs and sideboard
Maple with bog oak splats and woven
horsehair upholstery.
Table: 1520 x 1520mm / 60 x 60 in.

Extending dining table and chairs
Brown and bog oak.
1225 x 2340 to 3740mm / 49 x 92 to147 in.

Library furniture
Designed and made for Jesus
College, Cambridge. White
stained ash and white leather.

(right)
Home entertainment cabinet
Holly with ebony stringing.
2650 x 950mm / 104 x 38 in.

Johnny Hawkes

Johnny Hawkes has had a long and eventful career in designing and making furniture. His enthusiasm for his work, his love of wood and his forward-looking optimism is reflected in his work by his adventurous designs and innovative use of traditional and modern materials. His best work has a sensuality of line and sculptural form that raises it above the level of a lot of modern furniture. His down-to-earth attitude and business-like approach to his work is a pleasant surprise for his clients.

"You choose the wood carefully, you put all of your affection into it, sometimes it has humour in it."
Johnny Hawkes

Light veneer screen
As many as ten screens can be linked together or three in a triangle with a centre light. Poplar and aluminium.
Each panel: 1820 x 400mm / 72 x 16 in.

'The Recession' table
A quivering hall table depicting the angst of losing a company during the recession. Ebony and tulipwood.
890 x 1350 x 400mm
35 x 53 x 16 in.

Sofa table
The weight of the ebony platen set below the glass, tries to diagonally splay the legs out. Restrained by a ball joint, the structure becomes rigid. Ebony and satinwood.
400 x 1000 x 700mm
16 x 39 x 27 in.

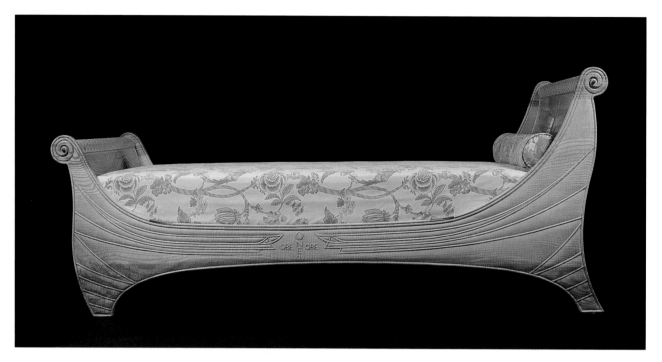

'The Obe One Kinobi' bed
Carved in deep relief throughout.
Ripple Ash.
950 x 2200 x 980mm / 37 x 87 x 38 in.

Honeymoon chaise
Tiger maple and silk taffeta.
1060 x 2200 x 1000mm / 42 x 87 x 39 in.
(Designed with Steve Pawsey)

'Diner Wave' chair
Designed for the four-hour lunch.
Solid teak.

'My Lover's Desk No.1'
Burry brown oak and bronze.
760 x 1600 x 810mm / 30 x 63 x 32 in.

'Croppy 5'
Screen signifying
the great crop
circles of 1996.
Bird's eye maple,
stainless steel
and magnets.
1830 x 400 x 25mm
72 x 16 x 1 in.

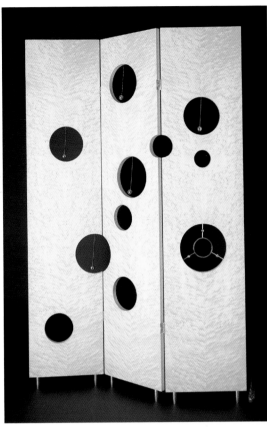

**'Gullwing'
spiral table**
Lacewood and
glass.
380 x 1000 x 700mm
15 x 39 x 28 in.

'Diner Wave' set
Inspired by boats, waves and sails from the bay at Cannes.
Teak and bronze.
Table: 760 x 2300 x 1400mm / 30 x 90 x 55 in.

'Spinal' chair
A chair for Merlin to dream
in and mix his potions.
Painted poplar.
1690mm high / 66 in.

Rave tables
Five fluorescent colours in
neon acrylic and psycho vinyl.
640 x 600mm / 25 x 24 in.

'Gullwing' chair
Designed to go with the Gullwing
spiral table. Blue sycamore and
leather.

Rachel Hutchinson

"My designs come about through experimentation; through getting a piece of cardboard or a piece of thin plywood, manipulating it into a form that I like and developing that into a piece of furniture. My aim within that is to be original as far as I can be, as aware as I am of what has gone before. I aim not to repeat but to innovate."

Rachel Hutchinson

'Martinsell' chair
Birch plywood and ripple sycamore.
780 x 600 x 600mm
31 x 24 x 24 in.

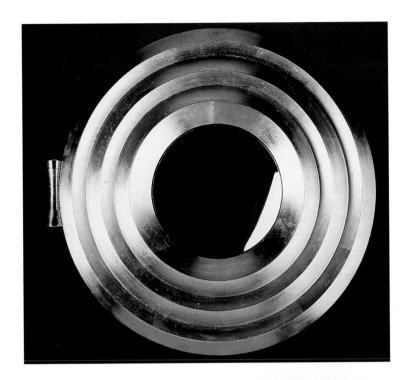

'Zero X' bathroom cabinet
Sycamore and gold leaf with
convex mirror.
150 x 600mm diameter / 6 x 24 in.

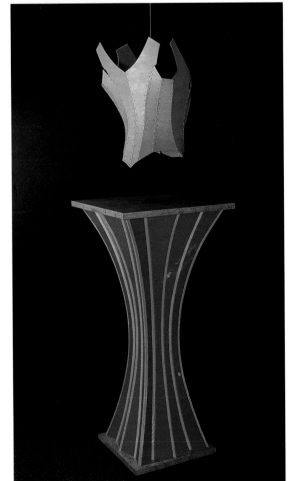

'Corset' pedestal
Ash and oak with plywood.
The upper corset hangs by
an almost invisible nylon
thread creating the
impression of the sculpture
suspended in mid-air.
900 x 420 x 420mm / 36 x 17 x 17 in.

Robert Ingham

'Quatrain' chest of drawers
Wenge and quilted maple with malachite pulls.
1370 x 400 x 400mm / 54 x 16 x 16 in.

Of all the furniture designer-makers who have started and remained successfully in business over the last twenty years, it would not be a gross exaggeration to state that the bulk of them were trained at Parnham College under the guidance of its principal Robert Ingham. Robert's exacting standards and patient guidance have been a major influence on a string of graduates that are now the backbone of the British designer-making industry. After twenty years at Parnham, creating furniture as and when his commitments would allow, Robert has now settled in a beautiful valley in North Wales designing and making furniture full time.

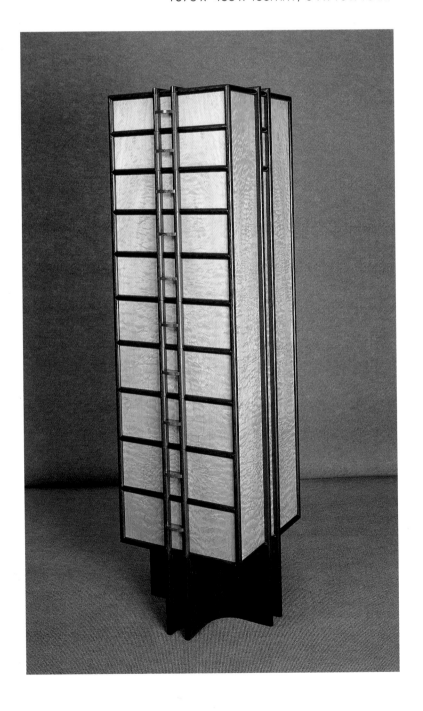

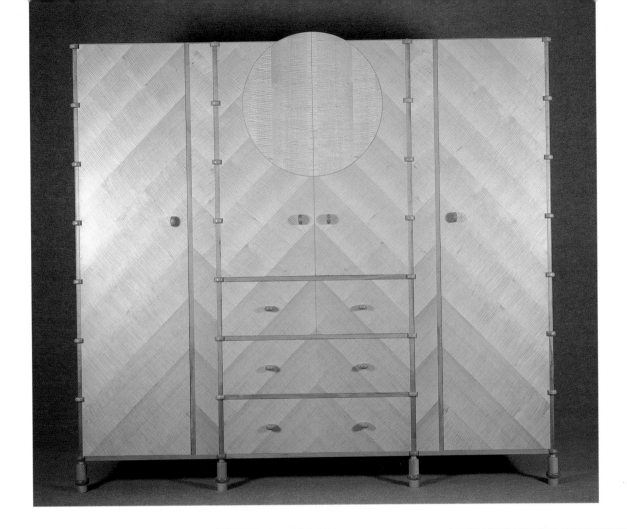

Wardrobe and dressing table

Swiss pear and weathered ripple sycamore.

Wardrobe:
1980 x 2440 x 610mm
78 x 96 x 24 in.

Dressing table:
1320 x 1370 x 510mm
52 x 54 x 20 in.

Dining/conference table
American red oak and burr oak.
2000mm diameter / 79 in.

Writing desk and stool
Bleached English oak and burr oak.
710 x 1220 x 460mm / 28 x 48 x 18 in.

Table with drawers
Swiss pear and weathered
ripple sycamore.
760 x 1000 x 430mm / 30 x 39 x 17 in.

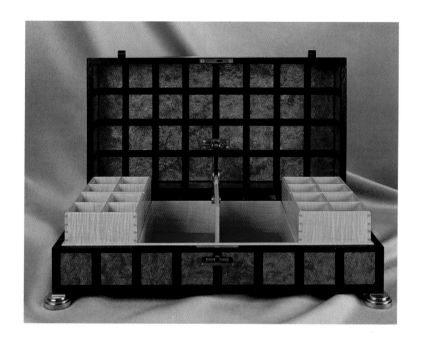

Treasure chest
Burr elm, bog oak and ripple
sycamore.
150 x 460 x 250mm / 6 x 18 x 10 in.

Jewellery box
Ripple and weathered
sycamore and purpleheart.
180 x 410 x 180mm / 7 x 16 x 7 in.

Trinket box
Wenge and burr ash.
50 x 180 x 180mm / 2 x 7 x 7 in.

Dressing table mirror
Wenge and amboyna.
670 x 740 x 260mm / 26 x 29 x 10 in.

'Curtsey' low table
Bleached wenge and burr oak.
460 x 920 x 920mm / 18 x 36 x 36 in.

Low table
Bleached wenge, bleached burr oak and patinated copper.
500 x 1070 x 1070mm / 20 x 42 x 42 in.

i tre

"The philosophy behind the making is as important as the actual design ...if you do not put quality and integrity into the work I feel the piece will not stand the test of time."

Petter Southall

The Highback Twist chair
Steam bent oak with Russia leather seat.
1500 x 500 x 500mm / 59 x 20 x 20 in.

For ten years Petter Southall built boats, specialising in the graceful Norwegian Oselver Faering. The making of this boat is an art passed from teacher to pupil - there are no plans. Now as a furniture designer-maker he adheres to the same traditional values.

The 'Olivia' china cabinet
The sides and elliptical arch are steam bent from 25mm/1 in. solid book-matched oak. Ripple oak, mouth-blown glass and leather.
2200 x 2450 x 450mm / 87 x 96 x 18 in.

Detail (right)
Cabinet handles in leather bound oak.

Adrian Jones

Originally trained in the aircraft industry, Adrian Jones followed his heart when he sought a place at Parnham College to pursue his lifelong interest in working with wood.

"I think furniture ought to be about more than looks - it should also be about feel and evocative aromas - cedar and camphor wood, echoes of earlier times."
Adrian Jones

Credenza
Maple, thuya burr and leather with boxwood and ebony inlay.
1800 x 440 x 900mm / 71 x 17 x 36 in.

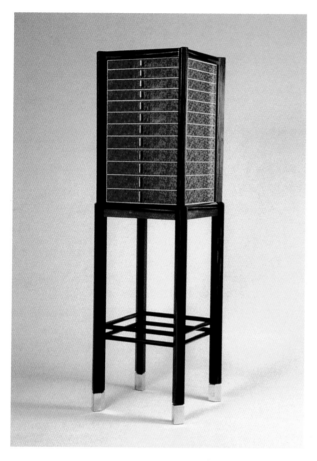

Collector's cabinet of twelve drawers
Macassar ebony, thuya burr, boxwood,
rippled sycamore, walnut and maple.
Bronze feet and handles.
1550 x 450 x 450mm / 61 x 18 x 18 in.

Display cabinet with integral lighting
American walnut and ripple cherry.
2200 x 1400 x 800mm / 87 x 55 x 32 in.

Prism low table
Macassar ebony,
bird's eye maple
and boxwood inlay.
360 x 1000 x 1000mm
14 x 39 x 39 in.

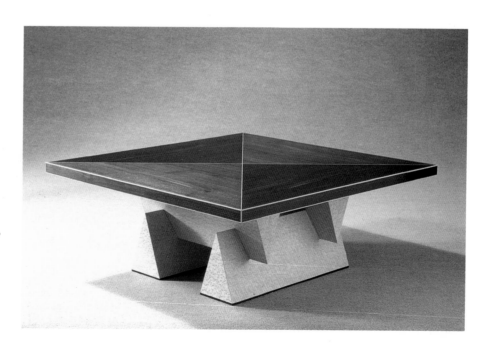

Philip Koomen

"...for creating is an expression of the human spirit in action."
Philip Koomen

Philip Koomen established his workshop in 1975 and employs a team of five craftsmen, including an apprentice. His work evolves from themes which may be based on traditional furniture or sculptural forms, but it is always designed to be appropriate to the client's lifestyle and practical needs. Although his furniture covers a wide price range, he aims to produce classic pieces that will become heirlooms for future generations. Above all, his work reflects his own deeply held spiritual beliefs and is made with passion and faith in the future.

Twelve drawer chest
English walnut with
boxwood inlay.
960 x 1170 x 580mm
38 x 46 x 23 in.

Dining table
Canadian rock maple.
1350mm / 53 in. diameter

Dining table and chairs
French oak with rosewood inlay.

Detail of sideboard
Bubinga and ebony.

Dining chairs
English brown oak with boxwood inlay.
910 x 450 x 450mm / 36 x 18 x 18 in.

Writing desk
Cherry, rosewood
inlay and stainless
steel.
730 x 1220 x 580mm
29 x 48 x 23 in.

Hi-fi cabinet
Cherry, bird's eye maple
with ebony inlay.
840 x 960 x 480mm
33 x 38 x 19 in.

Needlework cabinet
American black walnut with
boxwood inlay.
750 x 520 x 520mm / 30 x 20 x 20 in.

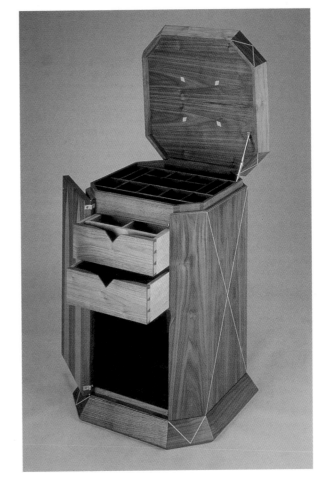

(Left) **Dining table and side table**
Dining table has an integral lazy Susan, shown in detail.
English walnut, burr walnut with ebony inlay.
Dining table: 1930mm diameter / 76 in.

(Left) **Bathroom interior**
Bird's eye maple, ebonised walnut and black granite.

'Pond Life' bench
Cedar of Lebanon.
2500 x 2500 x 690mm / 98 x 98 x 27 in.

Andrew Lawton

"Since I have been making furniture there has been a tremendous upsurge both in the number of good workshops and in the number of people who are interested in commissioning work. I think this is going to continue, especially as mass-produced furniture offers less and less individuality. Even more nowadays, people are becoming increasingly receptive to good design and are genuinely interested in pushing things forward."

Andrew Lawton

Hanging corner cupboard
Made of solid wych elm with bandsawn veneers.
810 x 460mm / 32 x 18 in.

Chest of drawers
Solid figured English walnut, maple, sweet chestnut and cedar of Lebanon.
1270 x 560 x 430mm / 50 x 22 x 17 in.

Library table
Commissioned for the
Richard Attenborough
Centre for Disability
and the Arts at the
University of Leicester.
American maple.
3500 x 1220mm
138 x 48 in.

'Chevron' writing table and chair
Derbyshire wych elm.
1370 x 560mm / 54 x 22 in.

Dining table
Seats ten. Maple,
bandsawn veneers of
bird's eye maple and
American black
walnut.
2000mm diameter / 78 in.

Lucinda Leech

Lucinda takes a serious environmental interest in the source of her raw materials and to this end has devoted much of her time to travelling extensively to research methods of managing, harvesting and the replanting of forests. This has given her the confidence to use exotic timbers in her work, when she is able to verify the source, and a variety of lesser known timbers to choose from. A young family has slowed Lucinda down a little over the past couple of years, but she is using the time away from the computer and bench to take stock, look at where she is going and to proceed renewed with a fresh approach.

Church furniture
For First Church of Christ, Scientist, Oxford. English ash.

(Left) **Conservatory table**
Tiger oak.
400 x 1000 x 500mm / 16 x 39 x 20 in.

Lawyer's desk Ash with laminated and ebonised birch.
740 x 2100 x 1200mm / 29 x 83 x 47 in.

Office furniture
Bubinga with black
lacquered details.
Cabinet:
2000 x 1000 x 500mm
79 x 39 x 20 in.

Display cabinet
Walnut.
2000 x 1100 x 400mm
79 x 43 x 16 in.

Detail of table under-frame
Bubinga, glass and marble with ebonised
detailing, showing the relationship between the
curves, emphasised by the use of opposing
colours in structural components and inlays.

Dining chairs
(from the left) American maple and walnut; English oak;
bubinga, ebony and leather; American cherry and
wenge; English elm and sycamore.

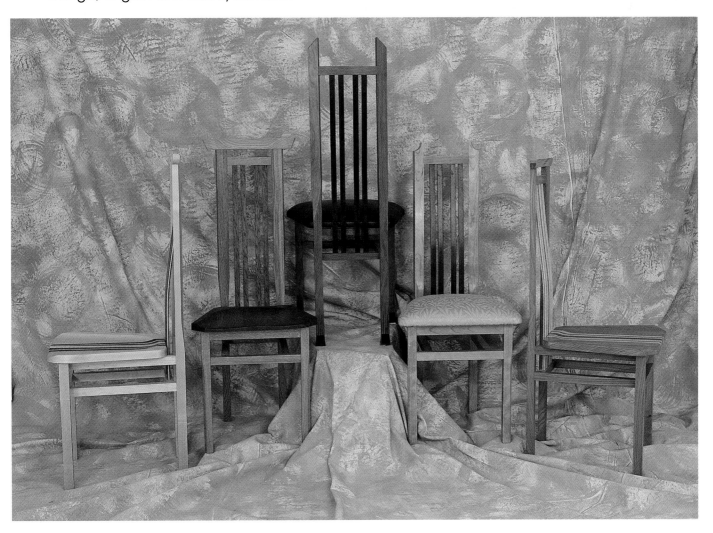

John Makepeace

John Makepeace is one of the few British furniture designers to achieve international recognition in his own lifetime, and one of the few in the world whose work commands prices comparable to fine art. Alone, he has done more to promote public awareness of the British furniture designer-maker industry than any other person or institution. His designs challenge the accepted boundaries and his workshops are continually experimenting to provide the innovative techniques required by these designs. To attend Parnham College, founded by John Makepeace in 1977, has been the goal of two generations of aspiring makers world-wide and his revolutionary experiment in the use of sustainable resources at Hooke Park is planned as a model for forestry and manufacturing in the new millennium.

'Arcade'
Detail of the side
of a chest of drawers
in cherry.

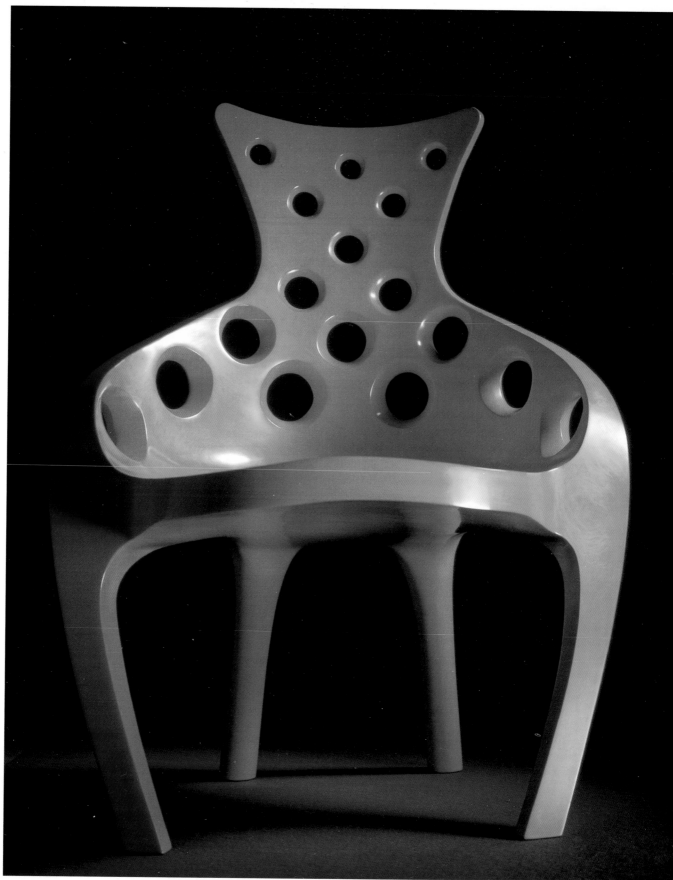

'Throne' Carved lime and burnished lacquer.
970 x 750 x 620mm / 38 x 29 x 24 in.

'**Vine**' Carved and coloured lime.

'**Agnes**' Pivoted gallery seat. Burr elm, coloured lime and cherry wood.

'**Millennium**' Laminated holly.

'**Swaledale**' Carved stool in lime and white gold leaf.

'Bird'
Burr elm, leather and cast bronze.
1100 x 1160 x 680mm / 43 x 46 x 27 in.

'Lunar' conference table and chairs
English cherry, burr elm, bog oak and leather.
7500 x 5000mm / 24ft 6 in. x 16ft 6 in.

'Time' dining table and chairs
Burr and plain 'weathered' oak.
Table: 720 x 3000 x 1500mm / 29 x 118 x 59 in.

Tony McMullen

Tony McMullen is one the last breed of makers who were apprenticed to the furniture trade, and trained in the art and craft of furniture making. He is steeped in the ethos of the Arts and Crafts movement and true to that tradition, he passes on his knowledge to the next generation at the University of Central England for a few hours each week, spending the rest of his time in his workshop. Tony is now experimenting with designs and techniques that will enable him to make furniture from materials not usually associated with 'fine' furniture.

Home entertainment cabinet
The central doors of the low cabinet pivot and slide back into the carcass for video and speaker access. Beech with sandblasted glass panels.
1700 x 3000mm / 67 x 118 in.

'Zig Zag' cabinet   Sycamore with parquetry doors of rosewood
and lacewood, rests on a stand of marble and aluminium.
1500 x 1500 x 400mm / 59 x 59 x 16 in.

Wall Unit
Oak and maple, with serpentine drawer
fronts and laminated shelves.
1800 x 3600 x 550mm / 71 x 142 x 22 in.

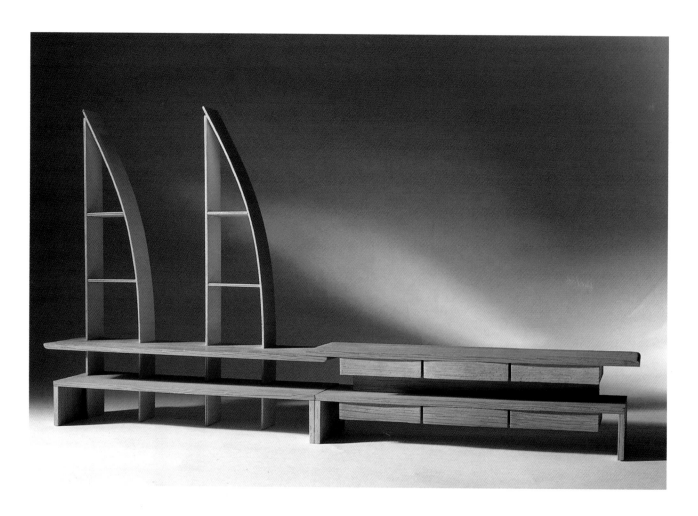

Table
2mm birch ply, sprung and glued into shape with glass top.
750 x 910mm diameter / 30 x 36 in.

Shelves
MDF, handpainted in acrylics with textured brush marks. These shelves have an oblique plan.
1800 x 300 x 300mm / 71 x 12 x 12 in.

Couch
Upholstered in leather on wood
laminate frame with foam infill.
2000 x 1320mm / 79 x 52 in.

Low table
Cantilevered top and legs in stained
and painted wood, with glass top.
430 x 1200 x 600mm / 17 x 47 x 24 in.

Gareth Neal

Gareth Neal describes himself as a functional artist, and his furniture as useful sculptures. His designs are based on natural organic forms where construction is secondary to form. This requires him to use creative alternatives to traditional methods in resolving technical problems.

"I hope that my designs will inspire the viewer and invite them into my imagination."
Gareth Neal

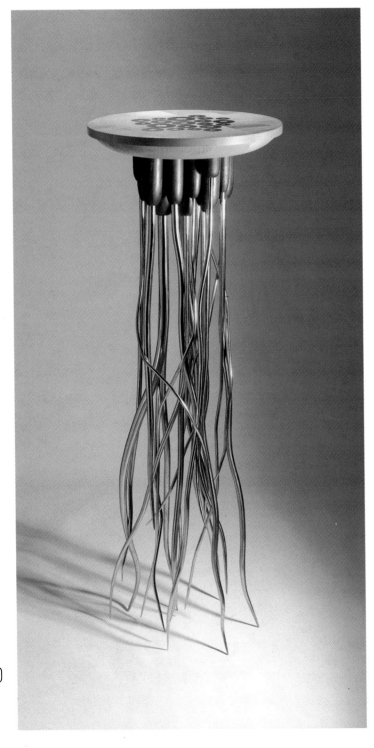

'Tendril' pedestal
Sycamore, walnut, silver and steel.
920 x 330mm / 36 x 13 in.

'Capillary' side table (facing page)
English oak.
810 x 810 x 350mm / 32 x 32 x 14 in.

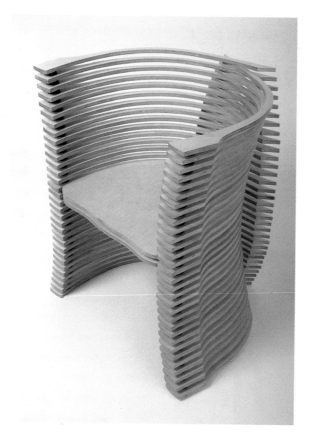

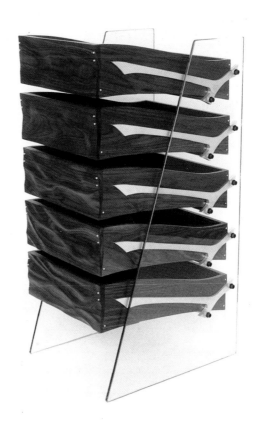

'Thoracic' occasional chair
Plywood with nylon detail.
910 x 430 x 410mm / 36 x 17 x 16 in.

Skeleton of drawers
Walnut, glass and aluminium.
970 x 430 x 510mm / 38 x 17 x 20 in.

Alan Peters

Alan Peters epitomises all that one expects of a craftsman; he is the revered elder statesman. Newly qualified designer-makers set out with the high ideal of possessing his quiet integrity. His clients will wait patiently until they head the top of his two-year waiting list. Throughout the fifty years that Alan has been involved in the industry his designs have moved confidently and inexorably towards the millennium. In 1990 he was awarded the OBE for his services to furniture design. Retirement, he tells me, is not part of his agenda and he is looking forward to producing his best work ever at a more leisurely pace.

Dining table and chairs
Indian sisso rosewood and sycamore. To seat ten.
Table: 737 x 2438 x 1168mm / 29 x 96 x 46 in.

Fan table
Solid sycamore and Indian ebony.
508 x 1220 x 508mm at centre / 20 x 48 x 20 in.

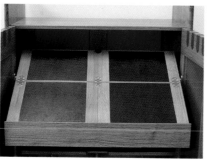

(above)
Cabinet interior.
(right)
Lectern in open
position.

Kelmscott Chaucer Cabinet

A tribute in solid Devon walnut to William Morris and exhibited at Morris' centenary exhibition. The cabinet holds a copy of Morris' Kelmscott Press edition *The Works of Geoffrey Chaucer*. 1422 x 890 x 406mm / 56 x 35 x 16 in. (Lettering by Tom Perkins and Ronald Parsons)

Nine Drawer Chest
Devon grown olive ash with detailing in Zambesi redwood.
1400 x 1016 x 457mm / 55 x 40 x 18 in.

Storage Cabinet
Solid walnut and bog oak.
1370 x 914 x 457mm / 54 x 36 x 18 in.

Six-seater dining table
Solid olive ash and bog oak.
1003 x 1980 x 991mm
39.5 x 78 x 39 in.

Tall cabinet
Yew with detailing in ebony and interior of ripple sycamore.
1422 x 483 x 241mm / 56 x 19 x 9.5 in.

Tub chair
One of a pair made in oiled Devon yew.
660 x 660mm wide
26 x 26 in.
(Upholstery fabric woven by Geraldine St Aubyn-Hubbard)

Gallery seating
For the Earth Gallery, Glasgow Museum of Modern Art, sculptured from home grown oak. 432 x 1725 x 710mm / 17 x 68 x 28 in.

'After Morris' dining table
Ash. 750 x 1320mm diameter / 29.5 x 52 in.

Coffer
Solid Devon walnut with
spalted door panels
from the same tree.
864 x 1830 x 610mm
34 x 72 x 24 in.

Low cabinet
Oiled tropical olive and
wenge.
533 x 1524 x 533mm
21 x 60 x 21 in.

Bureau
Bleached and natural oak with yew
interior.
1397 x 914 x 483mm / 55 x 36 x 19 in.

Silver chest (below right)
Devon walnut inlaid with stainless
steel.
1067 x 1067 x 508mm / 42 x 42 x 20 in.

Mushroom table
Made from the root end of a large walnut tree.
660 x 762mm diameter / 26 x 30 in.

Dining table
To seat ten. Walnut and cherry.
737 x 1829mm diameter / 29 x 72 in.

Low mushroom table
Walnut and sycamore.
406 x 838mm diameter / 16 x 33 in.

Octagonal occasional table
Sycamore, inlaid with padauk.
610 x 635 x 635mm / 24 x 25 x 25 in.

Nicholas Pryke

Nicholas Pryke comes from a background of structural engineering and architecture and this is strongly reflected in his work and his confident use of materials other than wood - stainless steel, glass, copper etc., and in the architectural roots of his designs. He spends the majority of his time at the drawing board, working closely with a network of top class craftsmen.

Corner cabinet
Vavona, etched glass and stainless steel.
950 x 500 x 500mm / 37.5 x 20 x 20 in.

Oval drawer pedestal
Burr ash, anodised aluminium and lignum vitae.   730 x 700 x 550mm / 29 x 27.5 x 21.5 in.

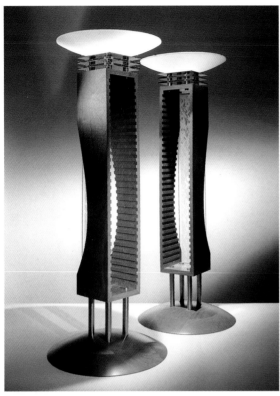

Folding coffee table
Canadian rock maple, stainless steel and
toughened glass.
400 x 1000mm diameter / 16 x 39 in.

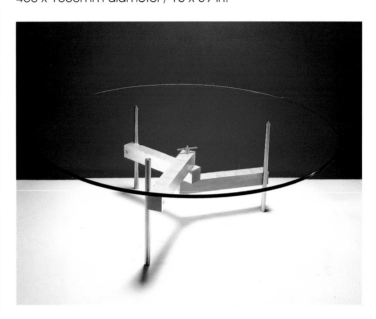

Compact disc racks
American cherry, hand etched glass, sandblasted
slumped glass bowl and stainless steel.
1000 x 350mm diameter / 39 x 14 in.

Coffee table
Layers of hand etched glass become
increasingly opaque with lower light levels.
Laminated oak, glass and stainless steel.
400 x 1200mm diameter / 16 x 47 in.

Dining table
The legs have been designed to
appear slightly anthropomorphic.
Aluminium, steel and ash.
740 x 1750 x 1100mm / 29 x 69 x 43 in.

David Savage

After six years of fine art training at the Ruskin School, Oxford and the Royal Academy, David Savage has spent many years in various fields of design and has been creating furniture since 1978. His inspiration is derived from organic forms, mainly plants and humans, and his designs evolve from a close rapport with the client. He is unable to work in a vacuum and this relationship, he considers, is essential to produce his best work.

"I am inspired by a client's confidence and trust. A piece is designed for that client, you can see them sitting on it, see them using it - that is what matters, their future enjoyment of it."

David Savage

Chaise longue (day bed)
Indian rosewood.
1200 x 1100 x 2100mm / 47 x 43 x 83 in.

Writing table and chair
Indian rosewood detailed with vavona burr and ebony.
750 x 1600 x 700mm / 30 x 63 x 28 in.

Desk chair
Rosewood with ebony detail. Back detail shows vavona burr panels.
1300 x 700 x 600mm / 51 x 28 x 24 in.

'Love chairs'
Each chair has its own identity. The male chair, on the left, is
stable, strong and dependable; the female of the pair is a free
spirit, carefree and energetic. English elm and ash.
1700 x 2300 x 1000mm / 67 x 91 x 39 in.

Hat stand
Swiss pear wood and Indian rosewood
detailed with rippled sycamore.
2000 x 900 x 600mm / 79 x 35 x 24 in.

Reception furniture
English oak and English brown oak.

Drinks cabinet
Pearwood.
800 x 1000 x 600mm
31 x 40 x 24 in.

Hall table
Indian rosewood.
800 x 800 x 600mm / 31 x 31 x 24 in.

Senior & Carmichael

"The hands-on element is very important to us because it improves our understanding of the pieces of furniture we can actually design. If we step aside from that we will never see all of the problems."

Charles Wheeler-Carmichael

Partners for twenty years, Rupert Senior and Charles Wheeler-Carmichael enjoy a challenge. They have always made the moving parts within their furniture, but for many years fostered an ambition to make a mechanically expanding table. One of their more adventurous clients threw down the gauntlet - "...if you can make it, I will buy it." All the work was done in their workshop and on completion this table was awarded a guild mark by the Worshipful Company of Furniture Makers.

Expanding mechanical table (Detail) The caps at the end of each of the bronze arms can be removed to allow candleholders to be attached.

Expanding mechanical table

American black walnut burr with mechanism of polished and patinated bronze and engine turned stainless steel. Seats six to ten. The table expands by turning the top. Eight leaves are then inserted into the spaces created.

Detail shows capstan closed.
740 x 1520 - 1880mm diameter
29 x 60 - 74 in.

Detail of Sun cabinet
Fluted sections of laminated ripple sycamore radiate from the burr yew centre of the sun, itself a secret drawer.

Sun cabinet
Ripple sycamore, ebony and burr yew.
2060 x 1160 x 390mm / 81 x 46 x 15 in.
(In association with A. Weston)

Expanding circular table
Figured birch, polished cast aluminium, masur birch and glass. The table extends by attaching an outer ring, made in eight sections.
Fantail dining chairs in maple with webbed and sprung upholstery.
Table: 740 x 1630 - 2000mm diameter / 29 x 64 - 79 in.

Detail
Shows the table top with central glass panel.

Side table
American black walnut.
840 x 1140 x 460mm / 33 x 45 x 18 in.

Display table
Sycamore and yew.
800 x 360 x 360mm / 31 x 14 x 14 in.

Hurricane and Lilliput chairs
Made in a combination of hardwoods salvaged from the 1987 hurricane.
Hurricane: 710 x 630 x 530mm
30 x 25 x 21 in.
Lilliput: 460 x 440 x 330mm
18 x 17 x 13 in.

Revolving bookcase
Walnut and wenge.
1300 x 570 x 570mm
51 x 22 x 22 in.

Detail
The independently rotating
lectern folds flat when not
in use.

S. F. Furniture

S. F. Furniture is a partnership of two well-matched makers. Ian Heseltine, the more serious of the two, and Declan O'Donoghue, the irrepressibly optimistic Irishman. They work successfully either together or alone as the mood takes them or as their clients demand. They come at design problems from opposite perspectives: Declan's approach is more conceptual, starting with the form and impact of the finished piece, using more than one variety of timber, assuming always that the piece can be built. Ian's approach is more technical, beginning with the function of the piece, how it will work and the making process, introducing the aesthetics as the design progresses, rarely mixing woods. Thus, two disparate elements that combine to make a unified whole.

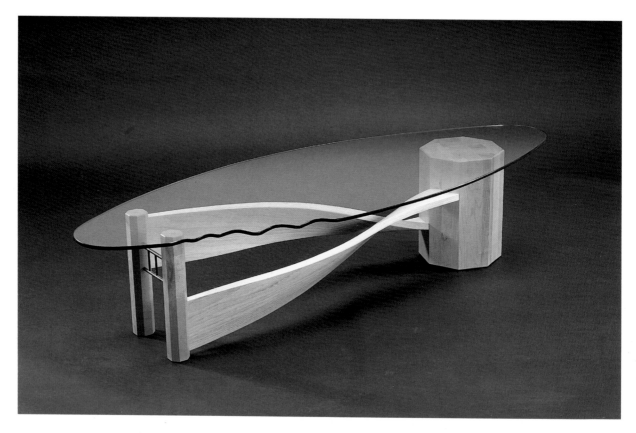

'**Meander**' An occasional table in laminated limed oak,
patinated brass, maple and glass. 400 x 1500 x 560mm / 16 x 59 x 22 in.

Occasional table
Bubinga with pearwood panels.
500 x 900 x 900mm / 20 x 36 x 36 in.

Collectors stereo cabinet
Ebony, burr vavona and satinwood.
1000 x 600 x 600mm / 39 x 24 x 24 in.

Dining chair
Imbuia, wenge and kevasingo.

Circular dining table
Brown oak.
2000mm diameter / 79 in.

Double Bed
Quilted maple and bubinga.

'Riverdance'
Foyer table in olivewood, recycled oak and glass.
600 x 2100 x 600mm / 24 x 84 x 20 in.

Bedroom chest
English elm, burr elm panels and handles.
700 x 1000 x 460mm / 28 x 39 x 18 in.

Bedside cabinet
Ripple maple and kevasingo.
800 x 700 x 400mm / 32 x 28 x 16 in.

Boardroom table
Cherry and burr madrona.
5000 x 3000mm / 16ft x 10ft.

Reception desk and curved lighting pillars
American cherry and granite.

**Sectional
boardroom table**
To seat thirty-five.
Ripple maple, burr
oak and aluminium.

'Plateau'
Public seating in Kilkenny limestone and oak.
2000mm radius / 79 in.

'Facet'
Public seating in polished and hand
chiselled limestone and elm.
4000mm / 13ft 2 in.

'Zenith'
Bench in weathered oak.
1800mm / 71 in.

'Tangent'
Convex and concave public
seating in oak and limestone.
2500mm / 98 in.

Prayer desk
Brown and burr oak.
900 x 560 x 400mm / 36 x 22 x 16 in.

Chapel furniture
Limed oak and stainless steel.

Altar furniture
Brown oak and white oak.

Bishop's chair
Brown oak and burr oak.

Silver Lining

"It is the satisfaction of knowing you have done a good job; the client feels it is value for money and that it is collectable."

Mark Boddington

Lectern
African wenge.
1270 x 480 x 430mm / 50 x 19 x 17 in.

Winning prizes for arts and crafts subjects at school encouraged Mark Boddington to take up a career in furniture making rather than following his father into the family business. Apart from a future in politics, one of Mark's goals is to make limited edition furniture which will make his work available to a wider audience, as he acknowledges that fine design and craftsmanship can be very expensive. In the meantime, his enjoyment at securing a commission from a difficult client is surpassed only by the return of a client for more work, be it in twelve months or twelve years.

Music cabinet
Burr and straight
grained walnut.
790 x 1570 x 500mm
31 x 62 x 20 in.

'Wishbone'
Low table in American walnut curl.
430 x 760 x 760mm / 17 x 30 x 30 in.

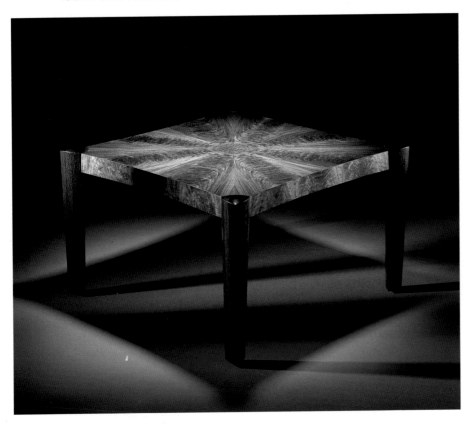

Clock
Walnut and silver.
210 x 100 x 50mm
8 x 4 x 2 in.

Commode
Amboyna burr, wenge, holly and leather.
1000 x 920 x 600mm / 39 x 36 x 24 in.

Maltese low table
Ebony and sterling silver.
450 x 610 x 610mm
18 x 24 x 24 in.

'Golden Sun'
Low table in amboyna with 9ct gold inlay.
610 x 610mm / 24 x 24 in.

Side table
Burr elm.
760 x 710 x 450mm / 30 x 28 x 18 in.

Sun Burst table
Walnut, satinwood and ebony.
720 x 1370mm diameter / 28 x 54 in.

Hall table
Ebonised mahogany.
720 x 1200mm diameter / 28 x 47 in.

'Lunar' side table (and detail)
Kingwood and sterling silver.
710 x 610 x 280mm / 28 x 24 x 11 in.

Paris club chair
Amboyna with hand woven chenille fabric.
760 x 760 x 760mm / 30 x 30 x 30 in.

'Wishbone' dining chairs
Cherry and sycamore.
990 x 510 x 510mm / 39 x 20 x 20 in.

Stemmer & Sharp

"To understand the unusual and make it into harmony is what I would like to achieve. In this world there are not enough things which are unusual but harmonious."
Andrea Stemmer

Andrea Stemmer was trained at Dusseldorf in Germany and at Parnham College. Her partnership with Fiona Sharp ended when Fiona died in 1995. Her work, mainly in solid timber from sustainable sources, displays clean sharp lines and is strictly functional.

Round table
Maple.   1750mm diameter / 69 in.

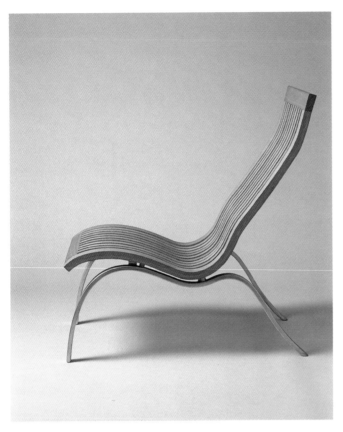

Garden lounger
Oak and stainless steel.
940 x 900 x 550mm / 37 x 36 x 22 in.

Tea table
Maple.
630 x 470 x 470mm / 25 x 18 x 18 in.

Round table (detail)

'Jekyll' garden table and curved bench
Oak.   800 x 740 x 1800mm / 32 x 31 x 71 in.

Trannon

"One does change the world - that is exactly what creative art is about - exactly why one is an artist - absolutely! absolutely!"

David Colwell

David Colwell is the designer at Trannon. It is his passionate belief that in an ideal world, wealth would be more equally distributed, resources would not be squandered and the environment would not be polluted. Well-managed forests would be planted and harvested to make fine furniture for ordinary people. To this end, Trannon makes batch production furniture from fast grown ash, making minimum impact on the environment and manufactured with a painstaking concern for pollution, energy conservation, fitness for purpose and retail price.

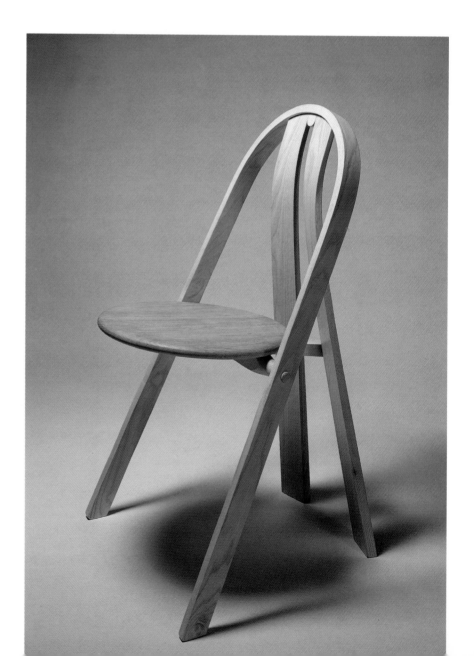

Recliner with footstool
Steam bent ash frame and rattan.

Stacking chair
Steam bent ash.

Captain's chair
Ash.

Writing desk
Ash.
800 x 1370 x 740mm
31 x 54 x 29 in.

Director's chair
Steam bent ash.

Extending table
Ash. Seats up to ten people.
The leaf is stored under the table.
1000 x 1600 to 2100mm / 39 x 83 to 63 in.

Cardiff sideboard
Ash.
750 x 1370 x 500mm
30 x 54 x 20 in.

Link bench
Oak and ash.

Cardiff Bench
Oak and ash.

Round table
Ash. Seats up to ten people.
1520mm diameter / 60 in.

High stool
Ash and stainless steel.

Settee with steam bent ash frame
The arms can be adjusted to three different positions.
900 x 1750 x 900mm / 35 x 69 x 35 in.

Andrew Varah

To meet this gentleman away from his workshop would give you no indication of the imaginative nature of his mind, but meet him in his design studio with photographs of his work on the walls and you begin to understand that commissioning from Andrew Varah could be fun. Like the currency broker who asked for his dining room furniture to reflect his profession. The client was presented with the drawings for the 'Card' table and chairs, perfectly encapsulating the element of chance in his occupation. The fun does not stop there, all significant pieces of furniture have a secret compartment containing an item of jewellery. Clients are given a year to solve the mystery, otherwise, rumour has it, Mr. Varah will reveal all and remove the prize.

Writing desk with infinity model housing stationery
Quilted maple and madrona burr. 1370 x 685mm / 54 x 27 in.

Double-sided desk
Cherry and pommelle mahogany.
1980 x 1066mm / 78 x 42 in.

Detail of drawer
Oyster cut yew.

Storage cabinet with infinity model
1680 x 610 x 610mm / 66 x 24 x 24 in.

Wardrobe
Satinwood and rosewood.
2133 x 2133 x 610mm / 84 x 84 x 24 in.

Cigar humidor
Oyster cut
laburnum and
yew.
177 x 300 x 200mm
7 x 12 x 8 in.

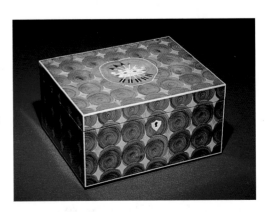

Collector's cabinet/desk with infinity model
Amboyna.   1860 x 950 x 750mm / 73 x 37 x 30 in.

Oak dining table and chairs
2590 x 1220mm / 102 x 48 in.

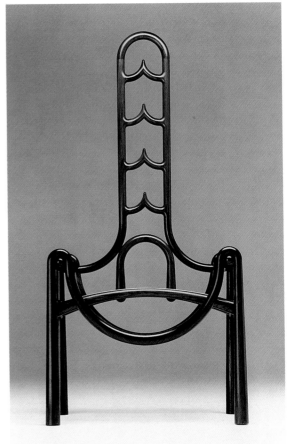

Solid rosewood chair
1370mm high / 54 in.

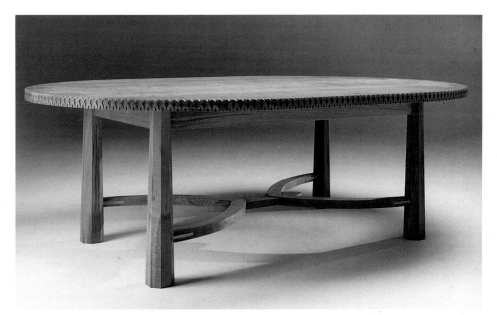

Dining table
Oak.
915 x 1830mm / 72 x 36 in.

CD cabinet
Cherry and rosewood.
900 x 1220 x 600mm
36 x 48 x 24 in.

Desk and chair
Myrtle burr and maple.
915 x 600mm / 36 x 24 in.

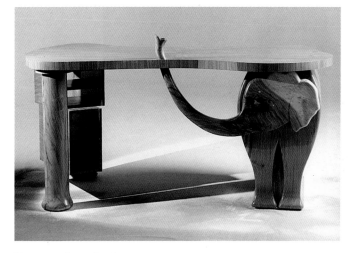

Computer desk
Walnut.   1220 x 760mm / 48 x 30 in.

Sofa table
Lacewood, black
walnut burr and holly.
760 x 1830 x 300mm
30 x 72 x 12 in.

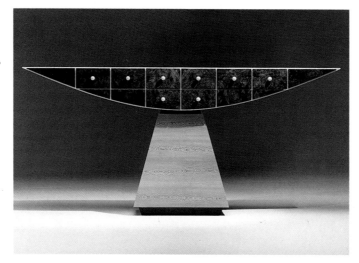

Occasional table
Bird's eye maple,
black walnut and
holly.
508 x 1066 x 406mm
20 x 42 x 16 in.

Bishop's throne
Beech.

**Kasparov chess
chair** (right)
Holly.

Sideboard
Madrona burr and fumed oak.
900 x 1525 x 600mm / 36 x 60 x 24 in.

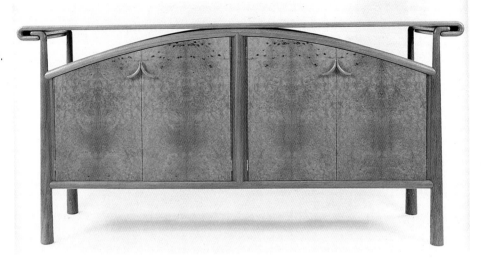

Dining table and chairs
Wenge and bird's eye maple.
2240 x 900mm / 96 x 36 in.

Marquetry 'Card table' and chairs
Pressure dyed woods.
2140 x 900mm / 84 x 36 in.

Dining chair
Solid cherry.

Wales & Wales

Rod and Alison Wales had been designing and making individual pieces of furniture for private clients for eight years when circumstances forced them to review all aspects of their business and redefine the focus of their interests. The resulting shift in direction towards corporate and architectural furniture has developed into a specialisation in atrium, museum and other public seating. They take particular satisfaction in the wider audience they are reaching and the effect on the public environment.

"There are issues to be addressed in designing and making furniture and we are doing our best to meet these demands. It makes for an interesting life's work."
Rod Wales

(Left) **Cabinet with nine drawers**
Natural and fumed oak with painted and
gilded details. First of the 'Stripe' series.
1680 x 420 x 320mm / 66 x 16.5 x 13 in.

(Above) **'Stripe' cabinets**
The second and third of the 'Stripe'
series. Natural and ebonised oak.
1440 x 520 x 365mm / 57 x 20 x 14 in.

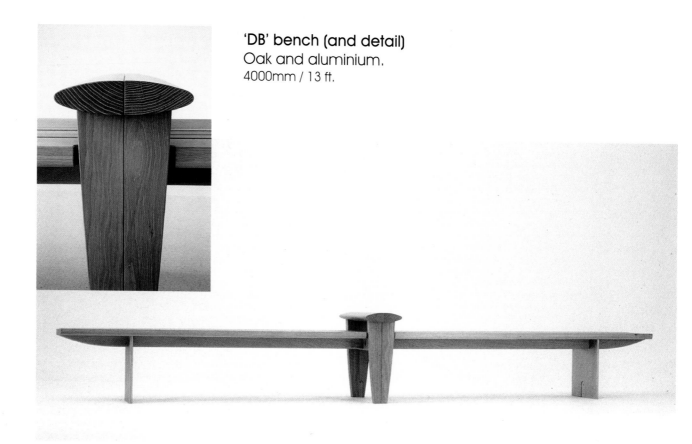

'DB' bench (and detail)
Oak and aluminium.
4000mm / 13 ft.

Water Gallery bench
Fumed oak and maple.
1500mm / 59 in.

'Smart Alex'
Beech and aluminium. A bench for anywhere.
Radii and sizes vary.

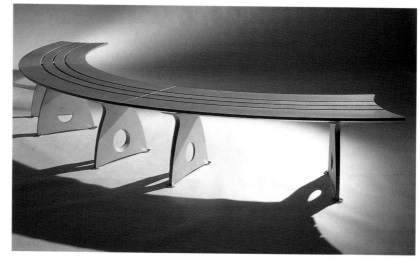

Boardroom table
To seat eighteen. Oak with bog oak detail. 4360mm diameter 14ft 4 in.

'Butterfly' chair
Beech.
(Designed by Wales & Wales, manufactured by Englender Furniture Ltd.)

'Leda'
Afrormosia and cast metal. Part of a range of street furniture.

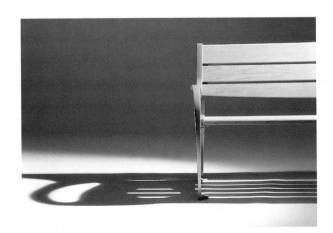

Shelf with two drawers
Sycamore, fumed oak, stainless steel and silver gilt detail.   1450mm / 57 in.

Cabinet with eight drawers
English oak, bog oak, 18 ct gold inlay. Height 1880mm / 74 in.
Detail (right)
Handle.

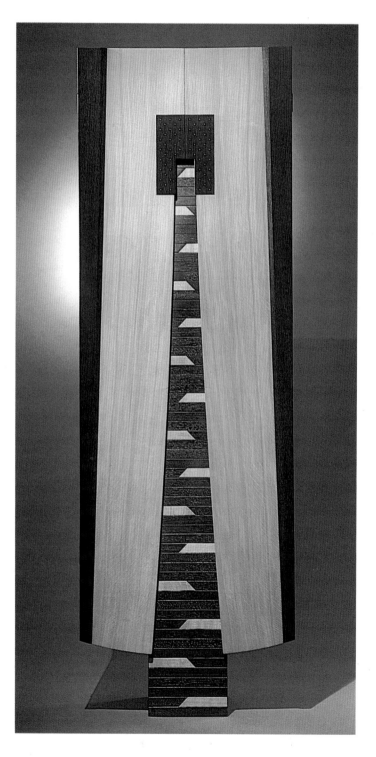

Waywood

"We have never tried to blow people's socks off with the first look at something, it is much more persuasive than that. A lot of customers have said this to us, that although they liked the piece when we first delivered it they liked it even more a year later, and that is the best thing that they could have said - it is what we are aiming for."

Barnaby Scott

Barnaby Scott and Clive Brooks head up the Waywood team whose furniture is made from solid home-grown wood and hand finished with natural oils and waxes. They employ a gentle philosophy to their work and demonstrate their concern for the environment by frequently planting new trees in the local landscape.

Chest of drawers
Dutch elm with carved beech drawer fronts.
910 x 510 x 160mm / 36 x 20 x 63 in.

Sideboard
Ash and olive ash with black walnut detail.
840 x 1830 x 480mm
33 x 72 x 19 in.

Sideboard with raised panels
Wych elm with quilted English elm panels and bog oak handles.
790 x 1680 x 510mm
31 x 66 x 20 in.

**Chairs with
laminated backs**
English and
brown oak.

Reception area coffee table
English oak.
2800mm diameter / 110 in.

Pair of bookcases
Tiger chestnut and sycamore.
1220 x 1980 x 410mm / 48 x 78 x 16 in.

Round dining table and chairs
Olive ash, brown oak and ash.
2080mm dia. / 82 in.

Elliptical dining table
Olive ash.
2540 x 1220mm / 100 x 47 in.

Sculptured chest
English oak and
burr elm.
560 x 1120 x 460mm
22 x 44 x 18 in.

King-size bed
Ripple redwood
with black walnut
detail.

Collector's cabinet
English and burr walnut.
1270 x 427 x 427mm
50 x 17 x 17 in.

Williams & Cleal

Justin Williams and Jane Cleal trained together at Buckinghamshire College and have worked in partnership since 1990. Their furniture, which is almost entirely for private clients, is designed by Jane and made by Justin. European and North American hardwoods are used with particular attention to sustainable resources.

'Tree' chair
Cherry and aspen.
970mm high / 38 in.

Sideboard
English cherry with ripple sycamore door panels and walnut beading.
810 x 1700 x 430mm
32 x 67 x 17 in.

Desk
English walnut, burr
chestnut and ebony.
800 x 1850 x 710mm
31.5 x 73 x 28 in.

Dining room interior
Steamed pear and burr maple
with ebony detailing.

Richard Williams

"I do not want to get dragged away from the bench, I would miss it too much."
Richard Williams

All well-run businesses grow, and Richard's was no exception. He no longer spent time at the bench; all his days were taken up with design work, meeting clients and watching his three cabinet makers make his furniture, until the day he saw a piece of furniture taking shape that he itched to be making himself. It made him realise that he wanted to do some of the making, but without a determined effort on his part he would never work at the bench again. Happily he solved the dilemma and now divides his time successfully.

Campaign table

African and Macassar ebonies, with holly inlay and a silver crest. The piece has a lid that lifts to provide a vertical notice board and to reveal a leather writing surface for the visitors book. The stand collapses and the entire piece packs into its own transit case for removal to camp.
890 x 1140 x 510mm / 35 x 45 x 20 in.

Pair of bedside tables

Honduras rosewood and lacewood burr veneer.
560 x 355 x 330mm / 22 x 14 x 13 in.

Bachelor's chest
Solid English oak and Australian walnut.
860 x 480 x 400mm / 34 x 19 x 16 in.

Sideboard
Solid English oak.
965 x 1520 x 460mm
38 x 60 x 18 in.

Occasional table
American black walnut.
Top and shelf in
sandblasted glass.
430 x 1100 x 610mm
17x 43 x 24 in.

Outdoor bench
Teak.
810 x 1780 x 640mm / 32 x 70 x 25 in.

Pair of wine tables
Macassar ebony, with drawers
in olivewood
690 x 330 x 250mm / 27 x 13 x 10 in.

Hall table
African and Macassar ebony.
840 x 910 x 330mm / 33 x 36 x 13 in.

Display cabinet
The piece has four drawers and is
designed to display a single
special item. English walnut.
1600 x 810 x 460mm / 63 x 32 x 18 in.

Rupert Williamson

Despite having a natural ability in the craft of furniture making, Rupert Williamson began his career using any other material except timber, rejecting wood because of its association with the brown colour of old furniture. Yet the inherent quality of wood to be manipulated appealed to him. Now he likes to use contrasting timbers such as maple and walnut which retain their colours and contrast strongly, emphasising form and structure. Spending less and less time at the bench, Rupert enjoys the challenge of designing furniture which reflects not only the client's interest and the brief, but combines, in a more abstract form, the geometry of man-made objects with the organic asymmetry of nature.

Dining table and six chairs
Sycamore and walnut with a
bronze structure.
Table: 1500mm diameter / 60 in.

Side table
Rosewood, inlaid
with boxwood.
800 x 500 x 500mm
31 x 20 x 20 in.

Desk chair (left)
Sycamore.
880mm high / 35 in.

Sofa table (far right)
Black burr walnut
and burr ash.
900 X 1700 X 400mm
35 x 67 x 16 in.

Side table
Storm damaged
Osage orange
wood from Royal
Botanical Gardens.
900 x 1800 x 400mm
35 x 71 x 16 in.

Dining table and ten chairs
Sycamore and walnut.   1200 x 1500mm / 87 x 59 in.

Anniversary table
Laminated maple with stained legs piercing the top.
6000 x 1200mm / 19 ft 8 in. x 4 ft.

Dining table
Maple with stained brackets.
1200 x 1200mm / 47 x 47 in.

Room light and paper bin
Sycamore and rosewood.
2800mm tall / 110 in.

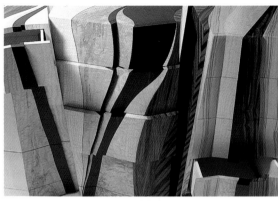

**'Rock' chest with
twelve drawers**
Variety of ten woods.
900 x 1800 x 600mm
35 x 71 x 24 in.

'Rock' cupboard
Variety of woods.
600 x 800 x 600mm
24 x 31.5 x 24 in.

Desk chair
Bog oak and sycamore
with leather seat.

Asymmetrical chair

Sycamore and redwood burr. This piece is a culmination of Rupert's interest in designing chairs from classical formats with organic imagery. It has no flat planes or right angles and is made of laminated components bolted on to the seat. The chair has been the ideal object for him to use asymmetrical forms, and with a relaxed functional seating position it becomes a three dimensional sculptural expression.
880mm high / 35 in.

Book table

Sycamore and walnut.
750 x 1200 x 1200 mm
29.5 x 47 x 47 in.

Jewellery cabinet

Rosewood and sycamore.
1400 x 800 x 400mm / 55 x 31.5 x 16 in.
(Silver enamel inlays by Jane Short)

Sideboard

Macassar ebony inlaid with silver.
900 x 1800 x 400mm / 35 x 71 x 16 in.

Toby Winteringham

Toby Winteringham's working life is split between his urge to design and his desire to make, and his furniture is similarly divided between, on the one hand the crisp clean-lined aesthetic with little or no decoration, influenced by the Shaker style and minimalist sculpture, and on the other hand by his more decorative work inspired by Biedermeyer, where motifs and patterns are applied usually in the form of marquetry inlay to a plain surface. "A constant quest" is Toby's description of his search for patterns with which to decorate his marquetry work. From an old hemp rope to a pebble lying in the sand, or a more unusual piece of chain, all of these items are photographed and decorate Toby's office - waiting for the right piece of furniture.

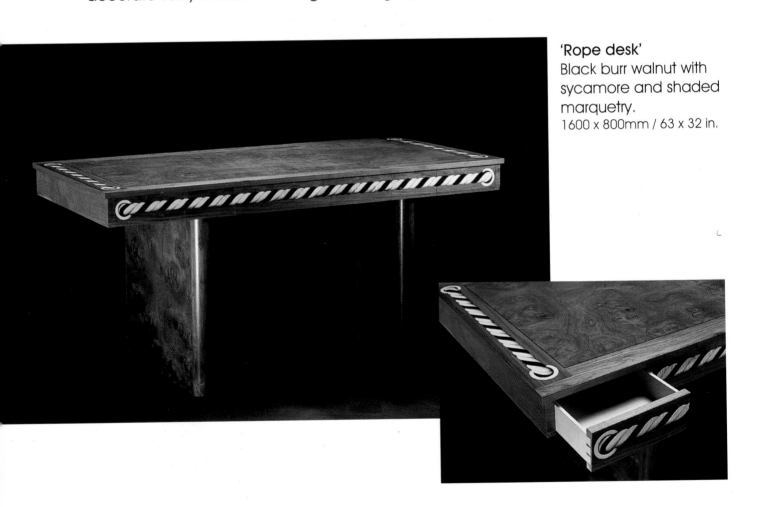

'Rope desk'
Black burr walnut with sycamore and shaded marquetry.
1600 x 800mm / 63 x 32 in.

Dining table and chairs
Inspired by Festival of Britain's 'Skylon'.
Elm and bubinga.
Table: 720 x 1800 x 950mm / 28 x 71 x 37 in.
Chair: 1070 x 480 x 480mm / 42 x 19 x 19 in.

'Solid' side table in ash
800 x 800 x 300mm / 32 x 32 x 12 in.

'Perseus' console table and mirror
English cherry with coloured and shaded marquetry and gilded cones.
Mirror: 900mm diameter / 36 in.   Table: 800 x 1200 x 500mm / 32 x 47 x 20 in.

Meeting table and chairs
Part of a complete office.
Elm and burr elm.
Table: 2000mm diameter / 79 in.

A small table top font
Elm with spun silver bowl.
300 x 270mm diameter / 12 x 11 in.

Detail of bed headboard
Rosewood, burr elm and
marquetry with ebonised
and gilded details.

Index of Designer-Makers

Mark Boddington
See Silver Lining

Clive Brooks
See Waywood

Matthew Burt
See Splinter Group

Ashley Cartwright
Elizabeth House
Weedon Lois
Towcester NN12 8PN
Tel/Fax: 01327 860056

Cato
133 Sylvia Avenue
Bristol BS3 5BY
Tel/Fax: 0117 977 9081

Jane Cleal
See Williams & Cleal

David Colwell
See Trannon Furniture Ltd

John & Louise Cropper
12 Newtown, Ipsden
Nr Wallingford
Oxon OX10 6AL
Tel: 01491 642196
Fax: 01491 641636

Detail
D2 Metropolitan Wharf
Wapping Wall, Wapping
London E1 9SS
Tel: 0171 488 1669
Fax: 0171 488 2524
gordon@detail.co.uk

Nicholas Dyson Furniture
The Close, Ardington
Wantage, Oxon OX12 8PT

Tel: 01235 834311
Fax: 01235 821392

Sean Feeney
The Old School
Preston on Stour
Nr Stratford on Avon
Warks CV37 8NG
Tel/Fax: 01789 450519

Paul Gower Furniture
10A West Street
Abbotsbury, Dorset DT3 4JT
Tel/Fax: 01305 871229

David Gregson
Bridge Green Farm
Gissing Road, Burston
Diss, Norfolk IP22 3UD
Tel: 01379 740528

Martin Grierson
22 Canham Road
London W3 7SR
Tel/Fax: 0181 749 5236
www.martingrierson.co.uk

Johnny Hawkes
See P W Ltd

Ian Heseltine
See S F Furniture

Rachel Hutchinson
1A Church Street
Pewsey, Wilts SN9 5DL
Tel: 01672 562936
Fax: 01672 564893
rachh@msn.com

Robert Ingham Designs
Bwlch Isa, Cwm
Dyserth, Denb. LL18 5SF
Tel/Fax: 01745 751101

i tre furniture
Chilcombe, Nr Bridport
Dorset DT6 4PN
Tel: 01308 482666
Fax: 01308 482433

Adrian Jones
1 Paulet Close, Hooke
Beaminster, Dorset DT8 3PD
Tel: 01308 863356
adrianj@globalnet.co.uk

Philip Koomen
Wheelers Barn,
Checkendon, Nr Reading,
Oxon RG8 0NJ
Tel/Fax: 01491 681122
www.koomen.demon.co.uk
furniture@koomen.demon.co.uk

Andrew Lawton
Goatscliffe Workshops
Grindleford, Hope Valley
Derbys S32 2HG
Tel/Fax: 01433 631754

Lucinda Leech
King Street, Jericho
Oxford OX2 6DF
Tel: 01865 510946
Fax: 01865 311842

John Makepeace
Parnham House
Beaminster,
Dorset DT8 3NA
Tel: 01308 862204
Fax: 01308 863806

Tony McMullen
Studio Workshop
Adleymoor, Nr Bucknell
Shropshire SY7 0ES
Tel: 01547 530878

Gareth Neal
105 Watersplash Road
Shepperton, Mx TW17 0EE
Tel: 01932 232214
Tel: 0498 672464

Declan O'Donoghue
See S F Furniture

P W Ltd
1 Church Street, Pewsey
Wilts SN9 5DL
Tel: 01672 562878
Fax: 01672 563043
www.i-i.net/p.w.ltd

Alan Peters
Aller Studios, Kentisbeare
Cullompton
Devon EX15 2BU
Tel: 01884 266251

Tony Portus
See Cato

Nicholas Pryke
1 Kingston Mews
Oxford OX2 6RJ
Tel: 01865 310400
Fax: 01865 316300

Gordon Russell
See Detail

David Savage Furniture
Makers
Rowden Farm, Shebbear
Devon EX21 5RE
Tel/Fax: 01409 281579
www.finefurnituremaker.com
dsavage@globalnet.co.uk

Barnaby Scott
See Waywood

Senior & Carmichael
The Whitehouse Workshop
Church Street, Betchworth
Surrey RH3 7DN
Tel: 01737 844316
Fax: 01737 844464

S F Furniture
Acton Turville, Badminton
Glos GL9 1HH
Tel: 01454 218535
Fax: 01454 218734
www.sffurniture.co.uk
d.od@virgin.net   i.an@virgin.net

Silver Lining
Aldford, Chester CH3 6HJ
Tel: 01244 620200
Fax:01244 620277
all@slwuk.com

Petter Southall
See i tre furniture

Splinter Group
Albany Workshops
Sherrington, Warminster
Wilts BA12 0SP
Tel: 01985 850996
Fax: 01985 850194
matthew@mbsg.freeserve.co.uk

Stemmer & Sharp
Oblique Workshops
Stamford Works, Gillett Street
London N16 8JH
Tel: 0171 503 2105
Fax: 0171 275 7495

Roy Tam
See Trannon Furniture Ltd

Trannon Furniture Ltd
Chilhampton Farm, Wilton
Salisbury, Wilts SP2 0AB
Tel: 01722 744577
Fax: 01722 744477
www.btinternet.com/~
trannonfurniture
trannon@btinternet.com

Andrew Varah
Little Walton, Nr Pailton
Rugby, Warks CV23 0QL
Tel: 01788 833000
Fax: 01788 832527
www.quartet.co.uk/av
avarah@quartet.co.uk

Wales & Wales
The Longbarn Workshop
Muddles Green,
Chiddingly, Lewes
E. Sussex BN8 6HW
Tel: 01825 872764
Fax: 01825 873197
rod@wales-and-
wales.freeserve.co.uk

Waywood
Butts Green,
Chadlington
Oxon OX7 3LT
Tel: 01608 676433
Fax: 01608 676291
www.waywood.co.uk
furniture@waywood.co.uk

Charles Wheeler-Carmichael
See Senior & Carmichael

Williams & Cleal
Willett Farm Workshop
Willett, Lydeard St Lawrence
Taunton, Som TA4 3QB
Tel/Fax: 01984 667555

Richard Williams
Unit 7, 28 Plantation Road
Amersham,
Bucks HP6 6HL
Tel: 01494 729026
Fax: 01494 721169
rw.fcf@fsbdial.co.uk

Rupert Williamson
5 New Bradwell Workspace
St James Street,
New Bradwell
Milton Keynes MK13 0BW
Tel: 01908 221885
Fax: 01908 221144
www.users.globalnet.co.uk/~rupertw
rupertw@globalnet.co.uk

Toby Winteringham
Whitehouse, Bawsey
King's Lynn
Norfolk PE32 1EY
Tel/Fax: 01553 841829

Photographic Acknowledgements

Key:
P = Portrait, **T** = Top, **TL** = Top left, **TR** = Top right,
C = Centre, **CL** = Centre left, **CR** = Centre right,
B = Bottom, **BL** = Bottom left, **BR** = Bottom right.

p14: **P** David Cousins, **BR** David Gilliland, p15: **T** and **B** David Gilliland, p16: **T** David Gilliland, **B** Jim Lowe, p17: **T** Jon Stone, **BL** Jim Lowe, **BR** Jon Stone, p18: **TL** , **TR** and **B** David Gilliland, p19: **T** Celia Burt, **B** Jon Stone, p20: **P** Will Shields, p26: **P** and **B** Kurt Vickery, p27: **T** and **C** Kurt Vickery, p29: **T** Eddie Fawdry, **B** Kurt Vickery, p30: **T** and **B** Kurt Vickery, p31: **T** and **B** Kurt Vickery, p32: **BL** Haddon Davis Photography, p33: **T** and **B** Haddon Davis Photography, pp46 to 49: Chris Challis, p50: **T** Chris Wright Photography, **B** Chris Challis, p51: **T** Chris Wright Photography, **B** Chris Challis, pp52 and 53: Farquharson & Murless, p61: John Jorgenson, p66: **B** J Bigglestone, p67: **T** M Lawrence, **B** J Bigglestone, p68: **T** and **B** P Bergan, p69: **TL** and **TR** P Bergan, **B** J Bigglestone, p70: **T** J Bigglestone, p71: **T, C** and **B** J Bigglestone, p73: **B** Dominic Harris, p74: **P** Liverpool Daily Post, p80: **P** Dorset Evening Echo, **BL** and **BR** Farquharson & Murless, p81: **T** and **B** Max Alexander, p83: **TR** Farquharson & Murless, pp90 and 91: Stephen Hepworth, pp92 to 97: Chris Honeywell, pp98: **BR** and 100: **TR** Farquharson & Murless, p102: Christof Weber, p103: **BR** Georgia Glynn Smith, p112: **P** Alan Richards, p113: **TL** and **TR** Whitworth Gallery, **BL** Woodley & Quick, p117: **BR** Crafts Council, pp118 and 119: Graham Pearson, pp120 to 123 and 125: John Gollop, p126: **B** Stuart Brown, pp127 and 128 **B**: Stuart Brown, p130: **CL** Stuart Brown, p132: **B** Blantern & Davis Photography, p133: **BR** Keith Denning, p134: **TL** Blantern & Davis Photography, p136: **TL** Roy Hewson, pp138 to 140, 142 and 143: Andreas Vogt Photography, p141: Tracy Gibbs, p144: **B** Stephen Brayne, p145: **TL, TR,** and **BL** Stephen Brayne, **BR** Adrian Arbib, pp152 to 157: Paul Lapsley Photography Ltd, pp158 and 159: Michael Hemsley (Walter Gardiner Photography), p160: **TL, TR** and **BR** Michael Hemsley (Walter Gardiner Photography), **BL** Antonia Reeve, p161: **T** Antonia Reeve, **CL, CR** and **BL** Michael Hemsley (Walter Gardiner Photography), pp162 and 163: Michael Hemsley (Walter Gardiner Photography), p164: **P** John Treen, **BL** Josephine Scott, **BR** Chris Honeywell, pp165 to 168: Chris Honeywell, p169: **T** John Treen, **B** Chris Honeywell, p170: **CR** Ian Mason, p171: **T** and **BR** Ian Mason, pp172 to 177: Craig Brown, p184: **P** John Hansell.
Book jacket: **front cover** Farquharson & Murless, **back cover** Alan Peters, Robert Ingham, Paul Lapsley Photography Ltd, Michael Hemsley (Walter Gardiner Photography).

The remaining photographs are the copyright of the individual designers and the publisher acknowledges use of their material in the production of this book. Every effort has been made by the editor and publisher to ensure that the copyright holders of photographic material have been acknowledged. Any omissions are regretted and will be corrected in future reprints of this book on receipt of written advice to the publisher.

In the captions to the photographs the dimensions are shown with approximate metric and imperial units. Where appropriate they are given as height followed by width followed by depth.